Frommer's™

Naples &
the Amalfi Coast
day BY day™

1st Edition

by Nicky Swallow

WILEY

A John Wiley and Sons, Ltd, Publication

Contents

UK Publisher: Sally Smith
Executive Project Editor: Daniel Mersey
Commissioning Editor: Fiona Quinn
Development Editor: Don Strachan
Content Editor: Erica Peters
Cartographer: John Tulip
Photo Research: Jill Emeny

Wiley also publishes its books in a variety of electronic formats. Some
content that appears in print may not be available in electronic books.

British Library Cataloguing in Publication Data
A catalogue record for this book is available from the British Library

ISBN: 978-0-470-72120-9

Typeset by Wiley Indianapolis Composition Services

Printed and bound in China by RR Donnelley

5 4 3 2 1

A Note from the Editorial Director

Organizing your time. That's what this guide is all about.

Other guides give you long lists of things to see and do and then expect you to fit the pieces together. The Day by Day guides are different. These guides tell you the best of everything, and then they show you how to see it *in the smartest, most time-efficient way*. Our authors have designed detailed itineraries organized by time, neighborhood, or special interest. And each tour comes with a bulleted map that takes you from stop to stop.

Hoping to see the best of Neapolitan Baroque architecture, take a stroll down the colorful Spaccanapoli, discover the secrets of Naples' underground sites or learn how pizza should *really* taste? Wanting to know the best route up Vesuvius or how to avoid the crowds in Capri? Whatever your interest or schedule, the Day by Days give you the smartest routes to follow. Not only do we take you to the top attractions, hotels, and restaurants, but we also help you access those special moments that locals get to experience—those 'finds' that turn tourists into travelers.

The Day by Days are also your top choice if you're looking for one complete guide for all your travel needs. The best hotels and restaurants for every budget, the greatest shopping values, the wildest nightlife—it's all here.

Why should you trust our judgment? Because our authors personally visit each place they write about. They're an independent lot who say what they think and would never include places they wouldn't recommend to their best friends. They're also open to suggestions from readers. If you'd like to contact them, please send your comments our way at feedback@frommers.com, and we'll pass them on.

Enjoy your Day by Day guide—the most helpful travel companion you can buy. And have the trip of a lifetime.

Warm regards,

Kelly Regan

Kelly Regan, Editorial Director
Frommer's Travel Guides

About the Author

Nicky Swallow has lived in Florence since the early 80's when she spent several years playing the viola in the opera house. A country walk with a colleague introduced her to the glorious scenery and earthy delights of Tuscan food; it was the start of a lifelong passion for all things Italian. This is her second book about Naples but she is also the author of guides to Florence & Tuscany, Milan and Cape Town. She writes regularly for magazines and websites about Italy and, as a nod to her musical past, runs a chamber music festival in southern Tuscany.

Acknowledgments

My thanks to Donald Strachan and his background knowledge of Italy for being such a helpful and encouraging editor. Luca Moggi not only took the photos for this guide but drove me all over Campania, sharing meals and enthusiasm along the way. We met some wonderful people while we were traveling and they all, in their own ways, have contributed to the book. We can't wait to go back.

An Additional Note

Please be advised that travel information is subject to change at any time—and this is especially true of prices. We therefore suggest that you write or call ahead for confirmation when making your travel plans. The authors, editors, and publisher cannot be held responsible for the experiences of readers while traveling. Your safety is important to us, however, so we encourage you to stay alert and be aware of your surroundings.

Star Ratings, Icons & Abbreviations

Every hotel, restaurant, and attraction listing in this guide has been ranked for quality, value, service, amenities, and special features using a **star-rating system.** Hotels, restaurants, attractions, shopping, and nightlife are rated on a scale of zero stars (recommended) to three stars (exceptional). In addition to the star-rating system, we also use a **kids icon** to point out the best bets for families. Within each tour, we recommend cafes, bars, or restaurants where you can take a break. Each of these stops appears in a shaded box marked with a coffee-cup-shaped bullet ☕ .

The following **abbreviations** are used for credit cards:

| AE | American Express | DISC | Discover | V | Visa |
| DC | Diners Club | MC | MasterCard | | |

Frommers.com

Now that you have this guidebook to help you plan a great trip, visit our website at **www.frommers.com** for additional travel information on more than 4,000 destinations. We update features regularly to give you instant access to the most current trip-planning information available. At Frommers.com, you'll find scoops on the best airfares, lodging rates, and car rental bargains. You can even book your travel online through our reliable travel booking partners.

A Note on Prices

In the "Take a Break" and "Best Bets" sections of this book, we have used a system of dollar signs to show a range of costs for 1 night in a hotel (the price of a double-occupancy room) or the cost of an entree at a restaurant. Use the following table to decipher the dollar signs:

Cost	Hotels	Restaurants
$	under $100	under $10
$$	$100–$200	$10–$20
$$$	$200–$300	$20–$30
$$$$	$300–$400	$30–$40
$$$$$	over $400	over $40

An Invitation to the Reader

In researching this book, we discovered many wonderful places—hotels, restaurants, shops, and more. We're sure you'll find others. Please tell us about them, so we can share the information with your fellow travelers in upcoming editions. If you were disappointed with a recommendation, we'd love to know that, too. Please write to:

Frommer's Naples & the Amalfi Coast, Day by Day, 1st Edition
Wiley Publishing, Inc. • 111 River St. • Hoboken, NJ 07030-5774

15 Favorite
Moments

15 Favorite Moments

1. Da Michele
2. Via San Gregorio Armeno
3. Archaeological Museum
4. San Gregorio's Cloister
5. Teatro San Carlo
6. Ferry
7. Vesuvius' Crater
8. The Nastro Azzurro ('Blue Ribbon') Road
9. Hotel San Pietro
10. Umberto a Mare, Ischia
11. Greek temples, Paestum
12. Arco Naturale Footpath, Capri
13. Ischia's Thermal Springs
14. Piazza del Duomo, Ravello
15. Fattoria del Casaro, Paestum

Previous page: Greek temples at Paestum.

This guide covers one of the most colorful, vibrant, and interesting areas of Italy, home to world-class museums and archeological sites, extraordinary scenery, superb restaurants, and enough hidden gems to keep an agoraphobic happy for days. It was a tough job to single out just 15 highlights, but my favorite moments range from a genuinely awe-inspiring first visit to Naples' Archaeological Museum to a memorable al fresco seafood meal.

Da Michele's pizza is the best in town.

❶ Tucking into your first pizza at Da Michele in Naples makes you realize what pizza is all about. The Neapolitans make the best in the world; crusts are light and puffy and toppings are made with San Mazzaro tomatoes and real mozzarella. Da Michele may not go in for frills, but the pizza is fab. *See p 78.*

❷ Walking up Via San Gregorio Armeno around Christmas can't fail to put you in the holiday mood. From early December, this Naples street is chock-a-block with twinkling shops and stalls selling artisan-made Christmas crib figurines. *See p 20.*

❸ Visiting the Archaeological Museum in Naples for the first time is an experience not quickly forgotten. The collections of Roman sculpture and the ancient bronzes are unique; just look at those two

bronze athletes with their haunting eyes in Rooms 114–117. *See p 28.*

❹ Taking respite from the city chaos in San Gregorio's Cloister soothes the soul; it's hard to believe that such a peaceful spot can exist among the madness of the Spaccanapoli. *See p 48,* ❽.

❺ Waiting for the curtain to go up at Teatro San Carlo, one of Italy's premier opera houses. There's nothing more exciting for opera lovers than the moment when the lights go down; performances here will not disappoint. *See p 67.*

❻ Catching a ferry to the islands. Naples is an immensely rewarding and exciting city, but it is undeniably crazy. After a few days wandering its traffic-clogged, noisy streets, jump on a ferry for a taste of sleepy island life. *See p 144–149 (Capri),* *p 150–157 (Ischia), and p 158–162 (Procida).*

7 **Peering into Vesuvius' Crater** offers a lasting impression of the awesome power of nature. The short trek up to the rim of the only active volcano in mainland Europe also offers fabulous views, wild flowers, and birdsong. *See p 119,* **3**.

8 **Glimpsing the Amalfi Coast for the first time,** as you descend the Nastro Azzurro ('Blue Ribbon') road that runs over the mountain from Sorrento to Positano, gives a taste of what it is to embark on one of the world's famous coastal drives. The scenery becomes increasingly dramatic as the blue sea glistens far below. *See p 128.*

9 **Drinking sunset cocktails on the terrace of the Hotel San Pietro** is one of the more indulgent highlights of an Amalfi Coast tour. This celebrated hotel enjoys a setting second to none, clinging to the side of a cliff just east of Positano. Cocktails are served on the top terrace to a backdrop of the town's twinkling lights. Magic. *See p 139.*

San Gregorio's Cloister; one of the most tranquil spots in Naples.

10 **Dining alfresco** on the freshest fish and seafood is the culinary highlight of a trip to these parts. Book a table at Umberto a Mare in Ischia; not only is the food fabulous, but also the terrace faces west, and so dinner is served as the orangey-red sun sinks into the sea. *See p 157.*

11 **The first view of the Greek temples at Paestum** is truly memorable. Some of the best preserved Doric temples outside Greece, Paestum's three giants rise from the surrounding countryside like a mirage. Try and catch them at sunset. *See p 120.*

12 **Walking the Arco Naturale Footpath on Capri** requires good shoes and plenty of stamina to cope with the 800-odd steps. But you will be rewarded by some of the most spectacular scenery to be found in the region. *See p 147,* **5**.

13 **Sinking into Ischia's warm thermal waters** on a cool spring or autumn day; the healing powers of Ischia's thermal springs have been known since Roman times. Perfect therapy for museum-weary bones. *See p 150.*

14 **An after dinner digestivo in Ravello's Piazza del Duomo** leaves the madness of the coast below far away. Refined Ravello is a civilized place to spend the night; after dark, the square, with its marble paving stones and lovely cathedral, is at its most atmospheric. *See p 103.*

15 **Tasting real *mozzarella di bufala* for the first time.** You don't know what mozzarella is until you taste the real thing; it bears no resemblance to the rubbery stuff you buy in those little bags at home. Produced by hand from buffalo milk, some of the best mozzarella in the world comes from the Naples area. The Fattoria del Casaro at Paestum makes its own. *See p 122,* **11**. ●

Strategies for Seeing the Region

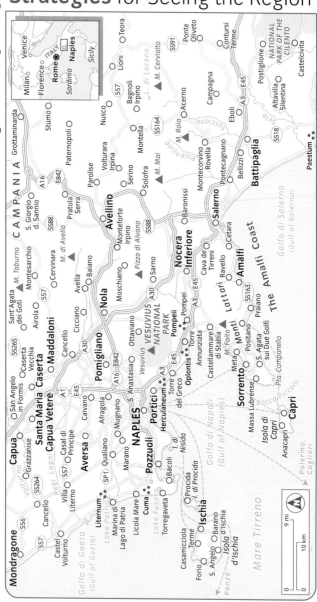

Previous page: Capo Miseno, Campi Flegrei.

There's a lot to see in this book: one of Italy's biggest cities full of extraordinary art treasures, a spectacular coastal drive, the many marvels of the ancient world, and mainland Europe's only active volcano. And I haven't even mentioned food, wine, lazing on the beach, or simply gazing at the scenery. Here are some suggestions for making the most of your time in Campania.

Al fresco lunch overlooking Borgo Marinari.

Rule #1: Don't push yourself too hard

Remember that you're on holiday and to go home a burnt-out wreck would defeat the object of the exercise. Naples is an invigorating but tiring city that's big, noisy, chaotic, and (in the summer) hot. So pick and choose what interests you most from Chapter 2, the 'Best of Naples'; don't try and fit too much into one day and leave plenty of time for breaks. The out-of-town tours are less stressful in that they involve smaller, quieter places, but these too get very crowded in the summer and traffic can be a nightmare. In short, don't take on too much.

Rule #2: Distances are short, but roads are slow

Apart from Paestum, which is around 100km (62 miles) south of Naples, all the places featured in this guide are quite close together. However, bear

in mind that the roads around the Sorrentine Peninsula and along the Amalfi Coast are narrow and, in the summer, clogged with traffic, so progress may be slow. The distances on Ischia and Procida are tiny, but again, the roads are often busy in high season. On Capri, you have to rely on your feet to get around, and so allow plenty of time.

Rule #3: Consider your method of transport carefully

Traveling by road in these parts can be slow going. If you're planning to stick to the towns, consider the train, boat, or a combination of the two. What could be more romantic than arriving in Positano at sunset and alighting on the beach? And what could be more infuriating than sitting at a virtual standstill several kilometers outside the town while you wait for two huge tour buses to squeeze past each other?

Procida's bustling port of Marina Grande.

Rule #4: Decide where to base yourself and whether to hotel-hop or stay in one place

Some people like to be based in one place and tour from there; others prefer an itinerant tour with a different hotel every night. Weigh up having to check in and check out, unpack and re-pack, each day against having to travel a little farther to see different places. If you plan carefully, you should be able to avoid too many hours in transit.

Rule #5: Take plenty of time for delicious meals

For me, mealtimes are an essential part of any vacation. I love food and find that the variation in food and food culture between regions is fascinating. *Mangiare* (eating) is very important in Italy, and nowhere more so than in Campania where the variety and quality of what's on offer is exceptional. A great meal needn't be expensive. Indeed, one of my most memorable gastronomic experiences while researching this guide involved a plate of deep-fried calamari, a wedge of lemon, a jug of ice-cold local wine, a plastic table cloth, and a beach. But if you're into gourmet meals, there's plenty of scope for those too. Picnics are also fun, and even the smallest village will have a *gastronomia* or *alimentare* (deli) where you can stock up on bread, cheeses, prosciutto, and other goodies. Do take time out in your day for lunch; Italy is all about taking things slowly and the Italians would never dream of skipping a meal.

Rule #6: Improvise

Use this book and its tours as a starting point for your adventures. Be brave, follow your instincts and whims, and explore. The locals in these parts are exceptionally friendly and if you get lost, they'll certainly help you back on track. Mix and match the tours according to your particular interests; choose a piece of one chapter, put it together with a chunk of another chapter, until you have your potpourri of a tour fixed. ●

The Best of Naples in One Day

Via Salvator Rosa

Via Correra

Via Pontecorvo

Via Montesanto

Via P. Scura

Cavour Ⓜ

Museo Ⓜ

Porta S. Gennaro

Via Carbonara

Piazza Museo

⑫

🏛 Galleria Principe di Napoli

Via Pessina

Via Pisanelli

Via Ruvo

Via Tribunali

Via Duomo

⑪

⑩

Piazza San Gaetano

Dante Ⓜ

Piazza Dante

Via Toledo

Porta Alba

⑬

Piazza San Domenico Maggiore

CENTRO STORICO

⑥ **⑧** **⑨**

Via B. Croce

ⓘ

⑦

S. Chiara

🏛 Musei Scienze Naturali

Piazza Nicola Amore

Università di Napoli

Corso Umberto I

Piazza Carità

⑤

✉ Posta Centrale

Piazza Matteotti

Via Medina

Via Depretis

Piazza Bovio

Via C. Colombo

Via Nuova Marina

Via Toledo

④

⑤

🏛 Galleria Umberto I

Piazza Municipio

Piazza Trieste e Trento

①

Piazza del Plebiscito

②

③

Via Acton

Molo Beverello

Bacino del Piliero

Stazione Marittima

ⓘ	Information
✉	Post Office
Ⓜ	Metro

SANTA LUCIA

Via S. Lucia

Via N. Sauro

Via Acton

Golfo di Napoli

0	1000 ft
0	300 m

① Gran Caffè Gambrinus
② Palazzo Reale
③ Castel Nuovo
④ Via Toledo
⑤ Gelateria della Scimmia
⑥ Gésu Nuovo
⑦ Santa Chiara
⑧ Ciao Pizza
⑨ Spaccanapoli
⑩ Pio Monte della Misericordia
⑪ Duomo
⑫ Museo Archeologico Nazionale
⑬ Intra Moenia

Previous Page: Crowds strolling on the Via Chiaia.

If you only have one day in Naples, you will have to work hard. This itinerary takes in Royal Naples' key sights, several of the city's great churches, a walk down colorful, crowded Spaccanapoli, and the world-famous Archaeological Museum. START: **Piazza Trieste e Trento.**

1 ★★ **Gran Caffè Gambrinus.** Start the day in the Grande Dame of Naples' cafés and erstwhile haunt of such celebrated clients as Oscar Wilde. Gambrinus has an impressive art deco interior with several cozy little salons for (expensive) sit-down coffee and cakes, and a big terrace out front. *Via Chiaia 1.* ☎ *081/417582. $–$$.*

2 ★★ **Palazzo Reale.** The size and splendor of this royal palace is fitting for a city that was once one of the most important in Europe. Inside lies a treasure trove of lavish baroque architecture and decor, which in its Neapolitan version is particularly sumptuous. The Spanish Viceroys commissioned the building, which was begun in 1600 by

Domenico Fontana (1543–1607), and then enlarged by the Bourbons in the 18th century. To see how the other half lived in those days, climb the monumental white marble staircase to the vast, lavishly-decorated Royal Apartments where there is an eye-popping collection of frescoes and paintings, chandeliers and furniture, all on display under a succession of gilded, stuccoed ceilings. Don't miss the exquisite 1768 theater and the Palatine Chapel with its elaborate nativity scene. ⏱ *1½ hr. Piazza del Plebiscito 1.* ☎ *081/ 5808111. www.palazzorealenapoli. it. Admission 4€ adults, 2€ EU citizens 18–25 yrs, free EU citizens under 18 and over 65. Mon, Tues, Thurs–Sun 9am–8pm (last admission 7pm). Bus 140, 152, R3, C4.*

Past kings of Naples stand in niches set into the façade of the Palazzo Reale.

❸ ★★ Castel Nuovo. Just north of the Palazzo Reale, the Castel Nuovo (known locally as the 'Maschio Angioino') seems in danger of being engulfed by the chaotic traffic system that encircles it. The castle is an important Naples landmark as well as the seat of the local government. Erected in 1279 by Charles I of Anjou, it was rebuilt by King Alfonso I of Aragon who added the splendid triumphal arch to mark his entry into Naples in 1443. The tall, narrow arch is fashioned in white marble, standing out sharply against the dark tufa stone of the rest of the fortress. Make sure you get up close for a good look at the detailed carving, carried out by some of the most eminent sculptors of the day; that's King Alfonso arriving above the main portal. Inside the castle, you can visit the Sala dei Baroni (today's council chamber), with its star-vaulted ceiling, and the starkly elegant Palatine chapel. The fresco fragments around the tall, slim windows in the apse are by Giotto; the walls were once covered with them. ⏱ 40 min. Piazza Municipio. ☎ 081/7955877. www.comune.napoli.it. Admission 5€ adults, 2€ EU citizens 18–25 yrs, free EU citizens under 18 and over 65. Mon–Sat 9am–7pm (last admission 6pm). Bus R2, R3, C25.

❹ ★ Via Toledo. This street (also, confusingly, called Via Roma) was once one of Europe's most elegant, lined with aristocratic palazzi. It is always teeming with people, especially during the early evening walk (passeggiata) when Neapolitans come out in force to stroll up and down, chattering, eating ice creams and window shopping. To the west of Via Toledo lies the notorious but colorful area known as the Quartieri Spagnoli, a dense network of narrow, rundown streets that couldn't be more of a contrast to the elegant retail heaven to the east. In spite of its reputation for petty crime, it's quite safe to venture in during the day, but do keep a tight hold on bags and wallets. ⏱ 30 min. Bus E6, R1, R2, C82.

❺ ★★★ kids Gelateria della Scimmia. Easily spottable thanks to the laughing brass monkey over the door, this old-fashioned place serves some of the best ice cream in town. Try the famous banana ice cream, half covered in chocolate. Piazza della Carità 4. ☎ 081/5520272. $.

❻ ★ Gésu Nuovo. Just east of Via Toledo in the eponymous

Via Toledo, also known as Via Roma.

18th-century majolica tiles decorate Santa Chiara's famous cloisters.

piazza, the church of Gésu Nuovo presents a severe façade to the world but hides an interior that's an exercise in baroque splendor. It was actually built as a palazzo in 1470, but converted into a church for the Jesuits in the late 16th century. The interior is a symphony of marble, gilt, and frescoes, topped by a barrel-vaulted ceiling. ⏱ *15 min. Piazza Gesù Nuovo 2.* ☎ *081/5518613. Free admission. Daily 7am–12:30pm and 4–7:30pm. Metro Dante. Bus E1, E2, R1, 201.*

❼ ★★★ Santa Chiara. Across the busy square from Gésu Nuovo, but a world away in terms of decorative style, lies the church and convent of Santa Chiara. It was built by Robert d'Anjou ('Robert the Wise') and his exotically named second wife Sancia di Majorca between 1310 and 1328 in the French Gothic style, and dedicated to the Poor Claires (*Les Clarisses*). Among the few works of art in the stark church, Robert's tomb is over the main altar. On either side, the tombs of Carlo, Duke of Calabria, and his wife Marie de Valois are exquisite pieces by the Tuscan sculptor Tino da Camaino (c.1285–1337). A visit to the adjacent cloister, known for its brightly colored majolica tiles, is a must; it's a rare peaceful spot in Naples. ⏱ *40 min. Via*

Benedetto Croce. ☎ *081/7971235. Free admission to church, 4€ for cloister. Daily 8am–12:30pm and 4:30–7:30pm. Bus C57.*

❽ ★ Ciao Pizza. For a cheap lunch on the hoof, order a slice or two of the excellent, freshly cooked pizza at this reliable fast-food joint. *Via B Croce 42.* ☎ *081/5510109. $.*

❾ ★★★ kids Spaccanapoli. You are now standing on what's probably Naples' most famous street. The pulsing, earthy heart of Naples literally splits (*spaccare*) the old city in

Spaccanapoli, the famous street that splits the old city in two.

The neo-Gothic façade of the Duomo.

⑩ ★★★ Pio Monte della Misericordia. This octagonal chapel, built in 1601 for a charitable institution, houses one of the most important paintings in Naples, Caravaggio's *Seven Acts of Mercy* (1607). The institution set out to help the poor by carrying out the type of acts illustrated in this seminal painting. Caravaggio's masterpiece demonstrates his characteristic chiaroscuro style in which light and shadow are played against each other. See also p 39, ❸. ⏱ *15 min. Via dei Tribunali 253.* ☎ *081/446944. www.pio montedellamisericordia.it. Free admission. Mon–Sat 9am–1pm. Metro Dante. Bus E1, E2, R1, 201.*

⑪ ★★ Duomo. The origins of Naples' cathedral are very ancient indeed, although you wouldn't know it from looking at the 19th-century 'Gothic' façade. Inside is the over-the-top Chapel of San Gennaro, which contains the remains of Naples' revered patron saint along with frescoes and numerous imposing bronze and silver statues of saints. Don't be so dazzled by all this that you neglect the rest of the church: there's a beautiful coffered ceiling, frescoes by Luca Giordano, and a superb Renaissance crypt under the high altar. You can enter the much smaller church of Santa Restituta and an underground archaeological area off the left aisle. Here, too, is the exquisite 5th-century baptistery of S Giovanni in Fonte. See also p 34, ❸. ⏱ *45 min. Via del Duomo 147.* ☎ *081/449097. www. duomodinapoli.com. Free admission (duomo), 3€ (archaeological area). Duomo: Mon–Sat 8am–12:30pm and 4:30–7pm, Sun 8am–1:30pm and 5–7:30pm. Cappella del Tesoro: Mon–Sat 8:30am–12:30pm and 4:30–6:30pm, Sun 8:30am–1pm; archeological area: Mon–Fri 9am–noon and 4:30–7pm, Sat and Sun 9am–12:30pm. Metro Cavour. Bus E1.*

two, following the line of the ancient Roman *decumanus inferior* (decumanus—a street running east to west); you can clearly see the division if you look down on the old city from the Certosa di San Martino (see p 18, ❶) or Castel Sant'Elmo (see p 18, ❷). Two further *decumani* run parallel to the north and it's around these streets and their north–south intersections (the ancient *cardines*) that many of the city's most famous churches and monuments are concentrated. Largely pedestrianized (although in this bewitchingly anarchic city this doesn't rule out the presence of flying scooters), the long street is a noisy, heady mélange of visitors, local shoppers, students, stalls selling tourist tat and religious souvenirs, book and antique shops, once-elegant palazzi, artisan workshops, fried food stalls, and homey restaurants. ⏱ *40 min. Metro Dante. Bus E1, E2, R1, 201.*

⓬ ★★★ **kids** **Museo Archeo-logico Nazionale.** Naples is home to one of the world's great archeological museums, which is particularly noted for its collection of Roman art and antiquities. Ideally, you should allow at least half a day to see and appreciate everything in there, but if time is limited, make a beeline for certain key works. Among the fabulous Roman sculptures on the first floor, look out for the mighty Tyrannicides, the *Farnese Bull*, the *Farnese Hercules*, and the bizarre, multi-breasted *Artemis of Ephesus*. On the mezzanine level are rooms filled with mosaics from Pompeii and Herculaneum and the Gabinetto Segreto, a fascinating collection of ancient erotica. The top floor is home to a remarkable collection of bronzes, both large and small; look out for the two Athletes and the head known as the Seneca. The glass collection on the same floor includes the famous Blue Vase from Pompeii. *See Museo Archeologico tour p 28.*

⓭ **Intra Moenia**. On shady Piazza Bellini, this literary bar has a terrace that makes a delightful spot for a well-earned cold beer or aperitivo. *Piazza Bellini 70.* ☎ *081/290988. $.*

Campania Art Card

If you're planning on 'doing' lots of sights in Naples and the surrounding area, it's worth investing in a Campania Art Card. Each card offers free or discounted entrance tickets for various museums, galleries, and archaeological sites and free public transport. There are several options, and so you need to work out which is most appropriate for your visit. The website explains it all clearly. You can purchase cards from bookstores, railways stations and the airport, the port of Naples, major hotels, travel agencies, and all the major sights.

If you stick to the itineraries outlined in the first three tours in this chapter (i.e., Naples in one and two days and the Campi Flegrei), purchase the 3-day card (16 €) that covers many of the sights mentioned plus public transport for the whole area. The first three museums/sights you visit are free and a 50% discount is offered from the fourth onward. For other combinations, see www.campaniartecard.it.

The Best of Naples in Two Days

Parco di Capodimonte

Piazza Ottocalli

CAPODIMONTE

Piazza G.B. Vico

Osservatorio Astronomico

Via Don Bosco

Salita Muradois

Palazzo Fuga

Orto Botanico

Piazza Carlo III

Salita Capodimonte

Via Miracoli

Via Foria

Corso Garibaldi

Piazza L. Poderico

Via Miracoli

Piazza Pagano

San Giovanni a Carbonara †

Via C. Rossaroli

Via M. d'Otranto

Via Casanova

Via Arenaccia

Ⓜ Cavour

Via S.G. Carbonara

Porta S. Gennaro

Piazza San Francesco

Via Pisanelli

Duomo †

Via Tribunali

Via Duomo

Piazza Capuana

Castel Capuano

Via Poerio

Stazione Centrale Ⓜ

Piazza San Gaetano

❼ ⓫

Piazza Garibaldi

❾ ❽

Piazza Mercato

Porta Nolana

⓬ ❻

Corso Umberto I

Corso Garibaldi

Via S. Cosmo fuori Porta Nolana

❿

CENTRO STORICO

🏛 Musei Scienze Naturali

Piazza Nicola Amore

Via G. Savarese

Piazza Mercato

Università di Napoli

Corso Umberto I

Via Nuova Marina

Piazza Bovio

Via C. Colombo

ⓘ Information

✉ Post Office

Ⓜ Metro

0   1000 ft
0   300 m

Your second day in Naples starts on a hill with one of the best views in the city and a visit to an ex-monastery complex turned museum. Then it's back to the center with a lively market and another dip into the *centro storico* to catch everything you couldn't fit in yesterday. Finish up at the Museo di Capodimonte. START: **Catch the Funiculare Centrale to Piazzetta Fuga.**

❶ ★★★ kids Certosa di San Martino. This sprawling complex of buildings (which includes a magnificent church, a cloister, museums and an art gallery, and terraced gardens) sits on a rocky promontory above the city with the waterfront and *centro storico* (historic center) laid out below; it's worth visiting just for the view. The church has a superb collection of 17th-century Neapolitan paintings and sculpture in its richly decorated interior. The peaceful Great Cloister encloses a smooth lawn planted with camellia bushes; in the corner is the monks' graveyard, topped with creepy marble skulls. The art gallery is housed in rooms built around the cloister; concentrate on the section that occupies the ex-Prior's quarters in the southern wing. Before leaving, pop in to see the famous collection of nativity cribs. ⏱ *1½ hr. Largo San Martino 5.* ☎ *081/5781769. Admission 6€ adults, 3€ EU citizens 18–25 yrs, free admission under-18s and over-65s; ticket includes Castel Sant'Elmo. Daily 8:30am–7:30pm. Funiculare Centrale to Piazzetta Fuga or Montesanto to Via Morghen.*

❷ kids Castel Sant'Elmo. Set just above the Certosa, this forbidding fortification, an ex-royal Anjou residence, dates from 1275. Now mainly used for exhibitions and concerts, it has worth great views over the city and Bay of Naples. To get back down to the center of town, catch the Funiculare Montesanto to the bottom of the hill. ⏱ *45 min. Via Tito Angelini 22.* ☎ *081/2294401. Admission 3€ adults, 1.50€ children. Thurs–Tues 8:30am–7:30pm. Funiculare Centrale to Piazzetta Fuga or Montesanto to Via Morghen.*

Monks are buried in the great cloister at the Certosa di San Martino.

The best views of Naples are from Castel Sant'Elmo.

3 **Friggitoria Fiorenzano.** This is a famous Naples 'frying shop' and a great place for a stand-up snack. The deep-frying is done in vats of boiling oil behind the counter; vegetables, bread dough balls, pizza, and *arancini* (rice balls) are served piping hot. *Via Ninni 1–3.* ☎ *081/5528665.* $.

4 ★★ **kids** **Mercato Pignaseca.** For a glimpse of workaday Naples, make time for a stroll around the colorful, chaotic Mercato della Pignasecca, where you can buy anything from fake Gucci sunglasses and pirated DVDs to a kilo of salt cod and some of the best mozzarella in the world. Centered on Piazzetta Montesanto, this is one of the city's oldest markets and the place to come for the best quality (and best value) produce. ⏱ *45 min. Piazzetta Montesanto and surrounding streets. No phone. Daily 8am–1pm. Metro Piazza Dante or Funicolare to Montesanto.*

5 ★★ **Bar Mexico.** According to many locals, this no-frills stand-up bar wins the award for the best espresso in town. A sign inside warns you that the coffee here comes pre-sugared. If you want it without, order *un caffè amaro.* *Piazza Dante 86.* ☎ *081/5499330.* $.

6 ★★★ **Cappella Sansevero.** Take Via Port'Alba, famous for its bookshops, back into the *centro storico.* Just to the south, one of Naples' most iconic works of art, Giuseppe Sammartino's *Cristo Velato* (Veiled Christ) is in this late 16th-century funerary chapel of the Sangro di Sansevero princes. The 1753 masterpiece, depicting Christ's body draped with a thin veil, stands in the middle of the chapel. The crypt contains a macabre example of Prince Raimondo's experimentations with embalming techniques. See also p 39, **2**. ⏱ *30 min. Via F dei Sanctis 19.* ☎ *081/5518470. www.museosansevero.it. Admission*

Friggitoria Fiorenzano.

Fabulouly fresh produce at the Pignasecca market.

6€ *adults,* 4€ *10–25 yrs, under-10s free. Wed–Mon 10am–6pm. Metro Dante. Bus E1, E2, R1, 201.*

❼ ★ Santa Maria delle Anime del Purgatorio ad Arco. You can't get into this 17th-century church, but have a look at the outside. The bronze skulls set on columns under the railings and the skulls and crossbones carved into the façade give a clue to the fact that the church was a center for the now officially banned death cult that gripped many Neapolitans for centuries. Followers of this cult would adopt the skull and bones of the dead, offering them gifts in exchange for good fortune. ⏲ *5 min. Via dei Tribunali 39. No phone. Metro Dante. Bus E1, E2, R1, 201.*

❽ ★★ kids Via San Gregorio Armeno. This street is famous for its shops selling *presepi* (Christmas nativity scenes). The art of making these intricate models with their dozens of figurines has been a part of Naples' artisan tradition for centuries and many of the workshops are here. During the Christmas period, the street is packed with people,

many of them locals buying additions for their family *presepe*. ⏲ *30 min. Via San Gregorio Armeno. Metro Dante. Bus E1, E2, R1, 201.*

❾ ★ San Gregorio Armeno. The church of San Gregorio Armeno and its adjacent convent was built in the 16th century on the site of a Roman temple, making its origins among the most ancient in the city. The interior, complete with an elaborate wooden ceiling and frescoes by Luca Giordano (1634–1705), is worth visiting as a fine example of the lavish Neapolitan baroque style. See also p 35, ❼. ⏲ *30 min. Via San Gregorio Armeno 1.* ☎ *081/5520186. Free admission to church; voluntary donation for cloister. Mon, Wed–Fri 9am–noon, Tues 9am–12:45pm, Sat, Sun 9am–12:30pm. Metro Dante or Montesanto.*

❿ Monte di Pietà. A charitable institution built this palazzo and chapel between 1597 and 1605. Two statues by Pietro Bernini (1562–1629) flank the entrance to the chapel; inside, the opulent Mannerist decorations include an elaborate barrel-vaulted ceiling. ⏲ *15 min.*

Via San Biagio dei Librai 14. ☎ *081/ 7913245. Free admission. Sat 9am– 7pm, Sun 9am–2pm. Metro Dante. Bus E1, E2, R1, 201.*

⓫ ★★ San Lorenzo Maggiore. One of the most important medieval churches in the city, San Lorenzo was built by Robert d'Anjou on the site of a 6th-century church. Its austere, barnlike interior contains some superb statues and monuments (most notably Tino da Camaino's 1323 tomb of Catherine of Austria) and an impressive cross-vaulted apse with nine side chapels. Perhaps the most fascinating part of the building lies beneath floor level in the Scavi di San Lorenzo (see p 34, **❻**). ⏱ *30 min. Piazza San Gaetano.* ☎ *081/2110860. www.sanlorenzo maggiorenapoli.it. Free admission. Mon–Sat 9am–5pm, Sun 9am–1pm. Metro Dante. Bus E1, E2, R1, 201.*

⓬ Gran Caffè Aragonese. Backtrack to Piazza San Domenico and this friendly bar/café with a large terrace at the top of the square,

where you can enjoy a cup of tea or a cold beer plus sweet or savory snacks. *Piazza San Domenico Maggiore 5.* ☎ *081/5528740. $–$$.*

⓭ ★★★ Museo di Capodimonte. Catch a taxi up Capodimonte hill to this deep pink and gray palace housing one of Italy's foremost art galleries. It's huge and so don't attempt to see it all; skip the lavish royal apartments, the porcelain and majolica, and the modern section, and focus on what the museum is famous for—its Renaissance and baroque paintings. When you're done, wind down with a walk in the pleasant, 7-sq.-km (3-sq.-mile) park. For a full tour of the museum, see p 42. ⏱ *1 hr, minimum. Via Miano 2.* ☎ *081/ 7499111. Admission 7.50€ adults, 6.50€ after 2pm, 3.50€ EU citizens 18–25 yrs, free for EU citizens under 18 & over 65. Thurs–Tues 8:30am– 7:30pm (last entry 6:30pm). Bus M4, M5, 178.*

Christmas cribs in Via San Gregorio Armeno.

The Best in Three Days

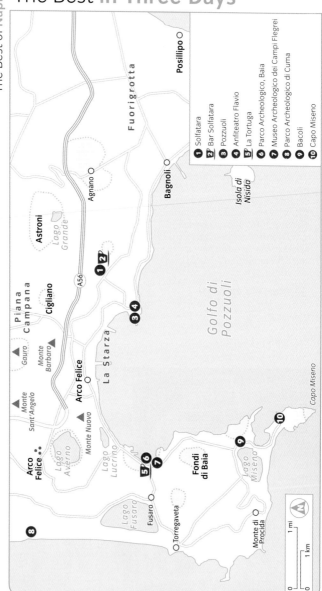

1. Solfatara
2. Bar Solfatara
3. Pozzuoli
4. Anfiteatro Flavio
5. La Tortuga
6. Parco Archeologico, Baia
7. Museo Archeologico dei Campi Flegrei
8. Parco Archeologico di Cuma
9. Bacoli
10. Capo Miseno

Having spent two hard days sightseeing in the city, it's time to get out for the day. This tour starts in Naples' western suburb and works its way farther west to the Campi Flegrei, roughly following the coastline, before finishing in Cuma. A car is the most convenient way to move around here, but the tour is also possible via public transport and a bit of legwork. START: **Solfatara.**

Hissing fumaroles at Solfatara.

1 ★★★ kids **Solfatara.** Start the day just east of Pozzuoli at the dormant sunken volcanic crater (770m/2550 ft in diameter) that the ancients called Forum Vulcani, believing it to be the residence of the god Vulcan. Extinct it may be, but the lunar landscape spews sulfurous steam that hisses out of the ground in jets, or fumaroles, that reach a temperature of 160°C (320°F). With the heavy stench of rotten eggs in the air, you can walk around the crater, stand in the clouds of steam, and marvel over the Bocca Grande, the largest fumarole; you will be given a helpful little map at the ticket office. At the center of the crater is the Fangaia, an area of hot mud that gently bubbles away at a temperature of 140°C (284°F). You can understand why the ancient Romans believed this to be an entrance to Hell. ⏱ *45 min. Via Solfatara 161, Pozzuoli.* ☎ *081/5262341. www. solfatara.it. Admission 6€ adults,*

4€ 4–10s yrs, free under-4s. Daily 8:30am–1hr. before sunset.

2 **Bar Solfatara.** There's a bar with a pleasant terrace just off the western side of the crater, where you can sit at a table under the trees and enjoy a cappuccino and brioche or a beer and a toasted sandwich. *Via Solfatara 61. No phone. $.*

From the entrance to Solfatara, turn right; a 15-minute walk down the hill brings you to the center of Pozzuoli.

3 ★★ **Pozzuoli.** Modern Pozzuoli is an active fishing and ferry port and hop-off point for the islands of Procida and Ischia. The town was founded by the Greeks in around 530 B.C., but became important only in the 3rd century B.C. St. Paul landed here in A.D. 61 on his way to Rome and in the town's Anfiteatro Flavia, San Gennaro (Naples' patron

The Roman macellum at Pozzuoli.

saint) was martyred by being thrown to the lions. Fast-forward a millennium or two and Sophia Loren was born in a Pozzuoli backstreet in 1934. Just above the port is the site of the Roman *macellum* (fish and meat market), lying below street level and known as the Tempio di Serapide. The site, with its jutting columns, is half submerged in water thanks to a strange geological phenomenon common in these parts known as bradyseism, effectively a rising and sinking of the level of the land. Above the port to the left is the original Roman settlement of Rione Terra where 18th-century palazzi were constructed over a warren of ancient roads, shops, and houses. 🕐 *1½ hr. Campi Flegrei Tourist office: Largo Matteotti 1/A, Pozzuoli.* ☎ *081/5266639. www. infocampifleigrei.it.*

❹ ★★ **kids** **Anfiteatro Flavio.** Pozzuoli's most spectacular sight is the c. A.D. 70–79 Anfiteatro Flavio, which, with its capacity of 40,000

Tickets & Transport to Campi Flegrei

By car, leave Naples on the well-signposted Tangenziale ring road towards Pozzuoli (18km/11 miles west). To reach the Solfatara and Pozzuoli by public transport, either catch city bus 152 from Piazza Garibaldi or the blue Sepsa bus (☎ 800 001616, www.sepsa. it), also from Piazza Garibaldi, which stops at Solfatara, Pozzuoli, and Baia. From the bus stop in the center of Baia, there are regular connections to Cuma and Bacoli. The itinerary here is a suggestion; you can easily change the order, or prioritize certain sites if time is short. Start early and move briskly, and it's possible to see the whole lot in a day. A cumulative ticket of 4€, valid for two days, covers four sites: the Anfiteatro in Pozzuoli, the Parco Archeologico and the Museo Archeologico in Baia, and the Parco Archeologico in Cuma. For more information, contact the **Campi Flegrei Tourist Information Office** in Pozzuoli (☎ 081/5266639; www.infocampiflegrei.it).

souls, was the third-largest arena in the Roman world. Although the huge oval seating area is impressive, the most remarkable features lie underground where, among the curving walkways, brick arches, and great chunks of columns and carved capitals, you can see the *carceres*, (cells) where exotic animals were kept for use in fight spectacles, and the long *fossa* (ditch) from where stage scenery was probably raised and lowered. ⏱ *20 min. Via Terracciano 75.* ☎ *081/5266007. Admission 4€ adults, free under-18s & over-65s. Wed–Mon 9am–1 hr before sunset.*

Anfiteatro Flavio.

5 ★★ **La Tortuga.** Located on the port at Baia with a terrace overlooking Vesuvius, this pleasant restaurant serves excellent dishes based on freshly caught fish and seafood. The spaghetti with monkfish arrives with the whole fish on the side. *Via Molo di Baia 42, Baia.* ☎ *081/8688878. $$.*

Baia lies about 7.5 km (4½ miles) west of Pozzuoli. Head north out of Pozzuoli on the SP 47; after about 1 km turn left onto the Via Campi Flegrei and follow the signs to Baia.

6 ★★★ **Parco Archeologico, Baia.** Unremarkable modern Baia gives little clue to the fact that ancient Baiae (named after Baios, the navigator of Odysseus) was one of the most fashionable and upmarket resorts in the Roman empire. Wealthy and powerful rulers (Julius Caesar, Nero, and Gaius) built villas here while thermal baths, temples, pools, and gardens stretched up the hill that overlooked the bay. Today much of ancient Baiae lies 7m (23 ft) underwater. Book a ride in a glass-bottomed boat to see the ruins, or don a wet suit and sign up for a diving tour. What remains of Baiae on

dry land can be seen at the Parco Archeologico, accessed from in front of the station. As you climb up the hill to the entrance, notice the large dome on your left; this is the so-called Temple of Diana, in reality part of a bath complex. Highlights include the eerily echoing Temple of Mercury with its intact dome (which pre-dates that of Rome's Pantheon), and a theater complex that some academics believe was a brothel. ⏱ *1 hr. Porticciolo di Baia.* ☎ *081/8687592. Admission 4€. Tues–Sun 9am–1 hr before sunset.*

7 ★★ **Museo Archeologico dei Campi Flegrei.** This unmissable Baia museum, housed in the 15th-century **Castello Aragonese,** commands splendid views of the bay. On the lower floor of the Torre Tenaglia is the reconstruction of a shrine to the cult of emperors, which once stood in nearby ancient Misenum; two of its original columns plus the carved architrave have survived. The statues at the back are of Vespasian and Titus and the 1st-century A.D. bronze equestrian statue depicts Domitian on a rearing horse. On the upper floor is the recreation of Emperor Claudius' nymphaeum, which was discovered in the Bay of Pozzuoli in 1959 and still lies there.

Baia's fascinating Archaeological Museum.

Statues from the complex were salvaged, however, and some are here including a headless Odysseus and two statues of a young Dionysus. Before you leave, climb to the top of the tower for the full impact of the panorama. 🕐 *45 min. Via Castello 45, Baia.* ☎ *081/5233797. Admission 4€, free under-18s & over-65s. Tues–Sun 9am–1 hr. before sunset.*

Cuma lies about 4 km (2½ miles) north of Baia; drive north on the SP45 following the signs for Cuma.

❽ ★★ **kids** **Parco Archeologico di Cuma.** The Greeks settled on the natural acropolis of Cumae in the 8th century B.C. The Romans expanded it, and built a long tunnel to connect to the nearby Lago di Averno, where they made an inland harbor. The place is surrounded by myth and mystery, being the home of the

The Burning Fields

The Campi Flegrei, the so-called 'Burning Fields,' is an extraordinary area of extinct volcanic activity and archaeological remains, both Greek and Roman, which lies to the west of Naples. It is steeped in myth, mystery, and weird geological phenomena: bubbling mud baths and hissing fumaroles, the cave of the Greek oracle Sybil at Cumae, the fabulous Flavian amphitheater at Pozzuoli, the submerged city of Baia, and the fabled entrance to the underworld at the Lago di Averno. It was here that Roman bigwigs built sumptuous villas, vast spa complexes, and mighty ports. All this acted as a magnet for the Grand Tourists in the 18th and 19th centuries, and although some of the romance has been swallowed up by ugly urban development, it's still a tour well worth taking.

fabled Cumaean Sibyl, one of the most celebrated oracles of her time who, it was believed, mapped out destinies. Virgil tells of Aeneas seeking help from the Sibyl to find his father in the underworld and describes her cave in Book VI of the Aeneid. You can see this cave for yourself in the park. Accessed down a long, narrow trapezoidal tunnel hewn out of the rock is the vaulted Cave of the Sybil, a fascinating, eerie, and otherworldly place where the prophetess is said to have sat and made her pronouncements. The park includes ruined temples to Apollo and, at the top, Jupiter. Although not much remains of either, it's worth climbing to the summit for the sweeping views and the highly suggestive atmosphere of this magical place. ⏱ *1 hr. Via Licola, Cuma.* ☎ *081/8543060. Admission 4€. Daily 9cm–1 hr before sunset.*

Drive back to Baia and take Via Bellavista, following the signs to Bacoli (7.4 km/4.6 miles).

⑨ ★ Bacoli. South of Baia lies the town of Bacoli, site of the Roman **Piscina Mirabilis** (the Exquisite Pool), a colossal, vaulted underground reservoir that was once part of a subterranean aqueduct system supplying water to the naval fleet at Miseno, to the south. The haunting atmosphere of the place is enhanced by the fact that few visitors get this far; you're likely to find yourself alone in the cathedral-like chamber. Caligula famously ordered a double row of boats to be floated across the bay from Bacoli to Pozzuoli, apparently in order to fulfill a prophecy that decreed he would only become emperor if he rode a horse across the bay. ⏱ *30 min. To visit, call the guardian* ☎ *081/5233199.*

Capo Miseno lies 6 km (3.8 miles) south of Bacoli and is well signposted.

⑩ ★ Capo Miseno. On the southern tip of the peninsula was the Roman Empire's most important naval base from where Pliny the Elder, commander of the fleet, watched Mt. Vesuvius erupt in A.D. 79. Today, Capo Miseno is a beautiful place with a marina and some good beaches. You can walk out to the tip of the peninsula for views that stretch to Naples, the islands, and Sorrento.

The mysterious Cave of the Sybil at Cumae.

Museo Archeologico

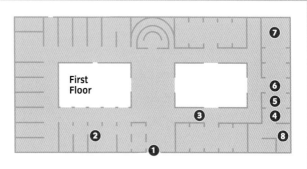

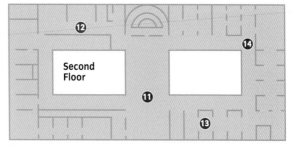

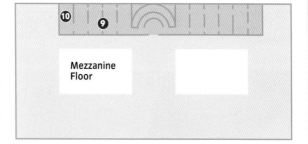

1. The Entrance
2. Roman sculpture in
   Campania (Rooms 30-45)
3. I Tirannicidi (Room 1)
4. Ercole Farnese (Room 11)
5. Artimede Efesia (Room 12)
6. Venere Callipige (Room 13)
7. Toro Farnese (Room 16)
8. Farnese Gem Collection
   (Le Gemme Farnesi; Rooms 9-10)
9. Mosaics (Rooms 57-64)
10. Gabinetto Segreto (Room 65)
11. Gran Salone della Meridiana
12. Villa dei Papiri (Rooms 114-117)
13. Wall Paintings (Rooms 66-78)
14. The Glass & Jewelry Collection (Rooms 85-89)

Naples' celebrated Archaeological Museum is home to the greatest collection of ancient art and artifacts in the world. A significant part of this was recovered from the sites at Pompeii and Herculaneum (both buried by Mt. Vesuvius in A.D. 79, see p 108 and p 114), while much of the rest is made up of the Farnese family's haul of Greek and Roman sculpture and other objects. START: **Metro to Museo. Trip length: two hours minimum.**

1 The Entrance. The museum entrance leads straight to the Atrium of the Magistrates where temporary exhibitions are held. Beyond that is the double marble staircase that climbs to the upper floors.

2 ★ Roman sculpture in Campania (Rooms 30–45). As a taste of what's in store, start off in the western wing of the first floor (wrapped around three sides of a courtyard), which houses a mixed bag of ancient sculpture found in the Campania region.

3 ★★ I Tirannicidi (Room 1). The Farnese collection starts in Room 1 which is dominated by the two powerful *Tyrannicides* (tyrant killers), 2nd-century-A.D. marble copies of renowned bronzes cast in 477 B.C. by Kritios and Nesiotes.

4 ★★★ Ercole Farnese (Room 11). At the near end of the long gallery of interconnecting rooms is this magnificent statue of Hercules, unearthed at the Baths of Caracalla in Rome in the mid-16th century. It is a signed Roman copy of Lysippus's 4th-century B.C. bronze.

5 ★★ Artimede Efesia (Room 12). This fantastical statue, carved from black basalt and yellow alabaster, shows *Artemis of Ephesus*; her multiple breasts symbolize fertility.

6 ★★ Venere Callipige (Room 13). Nothing could be more of a contrast to the monumental, masculine statues in this section than the graceful figure of Venus, another Roman copy of a Greek original that shows the goddess glancing shyly backwards at her

Roman statuary.

The Goddess Artemis.

reflection. It was found in Nero's Domus Aurea in Rome.

7 ★★★ **Toro Farnese (Room 16).** This colossal, powerful group sculpture, which stands at the end of the gallery, dates from the early 3rd century A.D. The largest surviving sculpture from antiquity, it influenced later sculptors such as Michelangelo and Giambologna.

8 ★ **Farnese Gem Collection (Le Gemme Farnesi; Rooms 9–10).** This collection (mainly composed of ancient cameos) is housed in two small rooms behind the Hercules sculpture. The star turn is the celebrated Farnese Cup, a delicate, translucent dish carved from several layers of sardonyx agate, made in Egypt during the Ptolemaic period (c. 330–300 B.C.).

9 ★★★ **Mosaics (Rooms 57–64).** An excellent collection of Roman mosaics takes up most of the mezzanine floor. They come in all shapes and sizes and mainly originate from Pompeii and Herculaneum. On the far wall is the huge, one million-*tesserae* (piece) depiction of the Alexander the Great during the Battle of Issus, dating from 125–120 B.C., which once lay on the floor in the Casa del Fauno (Pompeii, p 111). Look out for the exuberant bronze figure of the Dancing Faun, which gave the Casa del Fauno its name.

10 ★★ **Gabinetto Segreto (Room 65).** Closed to the public for years because it was considered too risqué for sensitive eyes, this collection of ancient erotica mainly comes from Pompeii and Herculaneum.

Museum Layout

The museum is laid out over four levels, in a vast 17th-century building that was once the seat of Naples University. To see it all in depth, set aside the better part of a day. If time is short, allow two hours and concentrate on the most important sections: the Farnese sculpture collection (inherited by Charles of Bourbon from his mother Elisabetta Farnese), the mosaics, the *Gabinetto Segreto,* and the collections of wall paintings and bronzes. If you have kids in tow, they will enjoy the Egyptian section in the basement, with its mummies, sarcophagi, and jewelry. Beware, however, that rooms and even whole sections are inclined to close without notice, due to restoration work or shortage of staff. If you visit on Sundays or public holidays, you stand the best chance of finding everything open.

The powerful Farnese Bull.

Certainly, some of the images on display in the paintings, mosaics, and sculptures are remarkably graphic, nowhere more so than the statue of Pan fornicating with a goat.

⓫ **Gran Salone della Meridiana.** The collections on the third floor are in rooms off this vast, frescoed hall, named after the zodiacal solar meridian that runs diagonally across the floor.

⓬ ★★★ **Villa dei Papiri (Rooms 114–117).** These rooms are dedicated to finds from the Villa dei Papiri in Herculaneum, most significantly the bronzes. Look out for the two lean Athletes poised for flight, the famous *Drunken Satyr*, lolling in a booze-induced stupor, the five life-sized female bronzes known as the Dancers, and the celebrated bust of Seneca, the Roman philosopher, statesman. and dramatist.

⓭ ★★★ **Wall Paintings (Rooms 66–78).** Off the far left-hand side of the Sala Meridiana lies the museum's unparalleled collection of wall paintings, found in Pompeii, Herculaneum, and the Vesuvian villas. The works offer an overview of the so-called Four Styles of Roman Painting (dating from around the 2nd century B.C. to the late 1st/early 2nd century A.D.) accompanied by clear explanation panels, also in English.

⓮ ★ **The Glass & Jewelry Collection (Rooms 85–89).** In pride of place in the center of Room 85 stands the 1st century A.D. Blue Vase from Pompeii, an exquisite treasure unearthed in Pompeii. Other cases contain examples of ancient decorative arts: glass, jewelry, silverware, and small bronzes.

Practical Matters

The Museo Archeologico is at Piazza Museo Nazionale 19 (☎ 081/4422111). Admission is 6.50€ adults, 3.25€ EU citizens 18 to 25 yrs, free for EU citizens under 18 or over 65. It's open Wednesday to Monday from 9am to 8pm (last admission 7pm); closed New Year's Day, 1 May, and Christmas Day.

Naples' Best Churches

1. San Giovanni a Carbonara
2. Santa Maria Donnaregina Vecchia
3. Duomo
4. Pastisseira Capriccio di Salvatore Capparelli
5. Basilica di San Paolo Maggiore
6. San Lorenzo Maggiore
7. San Gregorio Armeno
8. Berevino
9. Santa Chiara
10. Gesù Nuovo
11. Sant'Anna dei Lombardi
12. Certosa di San Martino

Naples is home to a remarkable number of churches that range in style from the Gothic austerity of Santa Chiara and San Lorenzo, to over-the-top examples of opulence such as San Gregorio Armeno. Baroque, in this city, is carried to its florid maximum. Earlier churches feature some remarkable sculpture while the 17th- and 18th-century buildings are repositories of the decorative arts. START: Metro to Piazza Cavour.

Little-visited San Giovanni a Carbonara.

❶ ★★ San Giovanni a Carbonara. Often overlooked by visitors (a big mistake), San Giovanni dates from 1339. It stands at the top of an impressive curving double stone staircase and houses some important Renaissance sculpture. Directly opposite the side entrance is the Miraballo family tomb (1519) by Tommaso Malvito, but it's difficult not to be distracted by the massive funerary monument to King Ladilas and his sister Joan II that towers almost 18m (60 ft) over the high altar. That's the King astride his horse, sword drawn, at the top. A door below the tomb leads to the circular, frescoed Caracciolo del Sole chapel with a rare majolica-tiled pavement dating from 1427. To the left of the high altar is another round Caracciolo family chapel, built entirely of marble. ⏲ *30 min. Via Carbonara 5.* ☎ *081/295873. Free admission. Mon–Sat 9:30am–1pm. Metro Piazza Cavour. Bus C58.*

❷ ★ Santa Maria Donnaregina Vecchia. This jewel of a church (now deconsecrated and used for exhibitions and concerts) is accessed through Museo d'Arte Contemporanea Donna Regina Napoli (MADRe; see p 40, ❺). The pleasingly minimalist Gothic interior contains the tomb of Queen Mary of Hungary, wife of Charles II d'Anjou, sculpted in 1323 by Tuscan Tino da Camaino (c.1280–c. 1337). Climb the altar steps and look back to see the nun's choir, whose walls are decorated with vivid 14th-century frescoes by Roman artist Pietro Cavallino (c.1240–c.1325). ⏲ *15 min.*

Queen Mary of Hungary's tomb in the church of Santa Maria Donnaregina Vecchia.

Via Settembrini 79. ☎ *081/5624561. www.museomadre.it. Admission 3.50€, free Mon. Mon, Wed, Thurs, & Sun 10am–9pm, Fri & Sat 10am–midnight. Metro Cavour. Bus E1.*

❸ ★★★ **Duomo.** Charles II d'Anjou built Naples' great cathedral, dedicated to San Gennaro, on the site of a 6th-century building that, in turn, stood next to the 4th-century Basilica di Santa Restituta, now part of the Duomo. Behind the unconvincing fake Gothic façade, the interior is impressive for both its size and splendor. On the right, the glittering Tesoro di San Gennaro houses the remains of the city's patron saint including two vials filled with his blood which, on the first Saturday in May, and then September 19 and December 16, miraculously liquefies (yes, really!). The nave of the church is crowned with a magnificent coffered ceiling. On either side of the main altar area, stairs lead down to the Renaissance marble *succorpo* (crypt) with intricately carved columns and a statue of Cardinal Carafa. The entrance to Santa Restituta is off the main church. Here you can buy a ticket for the archaeological area (see p 52, ❶) which also covers the tiny, not-to-be-missed Baptistery of San

Giovanni in Fonte, entered to the right of the altar. Decorated with dazzling 5th-century mosaics, it is the oldest building of its kind in the West. ⏱ *45 min. See p 14,* ⓮.

🍴 **Pastisseira Capriccio di Salvatore Capparelli.** This small bar/gelateria serves homemade ice cream and fresh, warm *sfogliatelle* (ricotta-filled pastries) from the bakery next door. Watch the city go by from the small terrace. *Via dei Tribunali 325.* ☎ *081/454310. $.*

❺ **Basilica di San Paolo Maggiore.** This vast church was built in the late 16th century on the site of a 1st-century temple to Castor and Pollux; those two massive Corinthian columns standing on either side of the entrance are from the original temple. ⏱ *15 min. Via dei Tribunali/Piazza San Gaetano.* ☎ *081/454048. Free admission. Mon–Sat 9am–noon. Metro Dante.*

❻ ★★★ **San Lorenzo Maggiore.** A favorite church of mine in Naples, the austere Franciscan appearance provides a perfect antidote to too much dripping gilt and inlaid marble. It wasn't always that way, however. The façade by

Ferdinando Sanfelice (1742) is all that remains of a baroque reworking of the original 13th-century church, started by Robert d'Anjou in 1265 on the site of a 6th-century church which, in turn, stood on the site of a Roman *macellum* (food market). Now back in its original form (thanks to postwar restoration), the wide, single nave is flanked by elegant Gothic arches and some fine tombs and sculptures. The florid baroque Cacace Chapel on the right stands out a mile in these bare surroundings. At the head of the nave, the intricately cross-vaulted apse with its nine side chapels is a magnificent example of Angevin Gothic. The monumental tomb to the right of the altar is that of Catherine of Austria, by Tino da Camaino (c.1323), its intricate marble carving inlaid with mosaics. *See p 21,* ⓫.

Baroque splendors at San Gregorio Armeno.

❼ ★★ San Gregorio Armeno.

Part of one of the most important convent complexes in Naples, the interior of this church stands out for its baroque decorations, paid for by the wealthy families of the nuns who lived here in its early days. The complex was built on the site of a Roman temple to Ceres, the goddess of fertility, in 1574. The interior is a strong contender for the most over-the-top example of Neapolitan baroque in the city, nowhere more splendid than in the lavish wooden ceiling, dripping in gold leaf. The church is famous locally for

Byzantine mosaics in the Baptistery of San Giovanni in Fonte, Duomo.

the cult of Santa Patrizia whose remains are in the chapel on the right of the main altar. Her blood liquefies on August 25 (her saint day) and each Tuesday. The peaceful convent cloister is a delight. *See p 20*, **9**.

8 ★ **Berevino.** Popular with students, this modern, stylish little wine bar serves a good selection of snacks such as platters of cheeses and cold meats and salads plus a good selection of wines by the glass or bottle. *Via San Sebastiano 62.* ☎ *081/290313. $–$$.*

9 ★★★ **Santa Chiara.** Santa Chiara's austere interior wasn't always that way. Started by Robert of Anjou in 1310, it was built in typical Provençal Gothic style but given a baroque makeover in the 18th century. It was restored to its original minimalist look after an Allied bombing raid in 1943; the resulting fire raged for six days causing devastating damage that left only the

exterior walls standing. Today, the interior is a serene, luminous space that provides a perfect setting for some fabulous Angevin funerary sculpture. The most important of these tombs, that of Robert himself sculpted in 1343–45 by the Florentine Bertini brothers, towers above the main altar. This is flanked by two works by the great Tino da Camiano; to the right is the tomb of Carlo, Duke of Calabria and to the left, that of his wife Marie di Valois, Tino's last work. Santa Chiara is famous for its tranquil cloister, entered around the left side of the church. *See p 13*, **7**.

10 ★★ **Gesù Nuovo.** The façade of Gesù Nuovo is unique among Naples' churches. Fashioned in dark basalt stone that has been formed into protruding pyramid shapes, it doesn't look as if it belongs to a church at all, and in fact, it was originally a secular palazzo, built in the 1470s but transformed into a church by the Jesuits in the late 16th century. Inside, every surface

Gesù Nuovo.

The unusual façade of Gésu Nuovo.

is covered with opulent baroque decoration; there is marble intarsia work on the walls, columns, and the floor, a magnificent barrel-vaulted ceiling, and paintings, frescoes, and sculptures by some of the greatest Neapolitan artists of the day. A quirky little feature lies in rooms off the right side of the church that are dedicated to Dr. Giuseppe Moscati, a miracle-performing doctor who was canonized in 1987. Ex-votos representing body parts hang floor to ceiling and there are reconstructions of his bedroom and study. *See p 12,* ❻.

⓫ ★★ Sant'Anna dei Lombardi. Lovely but little-visited, 15th-century Sant'Anna is a must for its magnificent collection of Renaissance sculpture. The Cappella Piccolomini (on the left) houses the carved tomb of Maria d'Aragona by Florentine sculptor Antonello Rossellino (1427–c.1479) and an anonymous painting of the *Annunciation.* Across the nave in the Mastrogiudice Chapel are altar carvings by another great Tuscan, Benedetto da Maiano (1442–1497). To the right of the high altar is an unusual *Pietà,* a life-sized terracotta group sculpture (1492) by

Guido Mazzoni; the stricken faces of the characters are believed to have been modeled on members of the Aragonese court. The Sagrestia Vecchia boasts a painted ceiling by Giorgio Vasari (1511–1574) and a set of intricate wood-intarsia stalls. Another of my favorites. ⏱ *30 min. Piazza Monteoliveto 44.* ☎ *081/ 5513333. Free admission. Tues–Sun 8:30am–12:30pm. Metro Montesanto. Bus E1, R1, R4.*

⓬ ★★ Certosa di San Martino. It's a little out of the way of the rest of the churches on this itinerary, but try and fit in a visit to this magnificent example of Neapolitan baroque style. Apart from the paintings and frescoes, the church has superb sculptures and marble intarsia work. Cosimo Fanzago (1591–1678) was responsible for the highly decorated chapel to St. Bruno and Giuseppe Sammartino (1720–1793) created the sculptures in the chapel of San Martino. In the sacristy (to the left of the choir) there are exquisite wood inlaid cabinets with panels illustrating scenes from the Bible, dating from 1587–1600. The Chapter House (to the right) has paintings by Carraciolo. *See p 18,* ❶.

Naples for **Art Lovers**

1. La Sfogliatella Mary
2. Cappella Sansevero
3. Pio Monte della Misericordia
4. Pinacoteca Girolamini
5. MADRe
6. MADRe Café
7. Certosa di San Martino
8. Museo di Capodimonte

i Information

✉ Post Office

Ⓜ Metro

Parco di Capodimonte

8 Museo di Capodimonte

CAPODIMONTE

Corso A. di Savoia

Salita Capodimonte

Salita Muradois

Osservatorio Astronomico

Via Miracoli

Orto Botanico

Via Foria

Piazza Sanita

MATERDEI

Materdei Ⓜ Via Materdei

Via M. R. Imbriani

Via S. Rosa

Via S. Rosa

Via S. Rosa

Via Correra

Via Pontecorvo

Piazza Mazzini

Via A. Villari

Piazza Pagano

Cavour Ⓜ

Via Rossaroli

Museo Archeologico Nazionale Ⓜ Museo

Piazza Museo

🏛 Galleria Principe di Napoli

Via Ruvo

Porta S. Gennaro

Via Carbonara

6 Via Carbonara

5

Via Pisanelli

Duomo ✝

Piazza Capuana

4

Via Tribunali

Via Duomo

Castel Capuano

Piazza San Gaetano

3

Dante Ⓜ

Piazza San Domenico Maggiore 2

CENTRO STORICO

Piazza Dante

Emanuele

Ⓜ Stazione 🚇 Montesano

Ⓕ

Piazza Montesanto

5

Via P. Scura

Via Toledo

Via B. Croce

1

i

S. Chiara ✝

Università di Napoli

Musei Scienze Naturali 🏛

Piazza Nicola Amore

Piazza Mercato

Corso V. Vittorio

Piazza Carità

Posta Centrale ✉

Piazza Bovio

Corso Umberto I

Piazza Matteotti

Via Nuova Marina

Via Toledo

Via Medina

Via Depretis

Corso Umberto I

Via C. Colombo

Bacino del Piliero

QUARTIERI SPAGNOLI

7

Galleria Umberto I 🏛

Ⓕ

Piazza Trieste e Trento

Piazza Municipio

Maschio Angioino (Castel Nuovo)

Stazione Marittima

Golfo di Napoli

Via Chiaia

Piazza del Plebiscito

Palazzo Reale

Via Acton

Molo Beverello

Via Acton

Piazza d. Martiri

SANTA LUCIA

0   1000 ft

0   300 m

A rt lovers are kept busy in Naples, home to one of Italy's premier collections of art housed in the Museo di Capodimonte. Seminal masterpieces are hidden away in chapels and small galleries, and paintings that survived the devastation of Pompeii are inside the Museo Archeologico. Naples is also gaining a reputation as a center for contemporary art. START: **Spaccanapoli.**

1 ★★ La Sfogliatella Mary.

There's no time for more than a quick, stand-up breakfast, so head for Mary's little street stall in the Spaccanapoli for a spectacular rum babà or a delicious ricotta-filled sfogliatella. *Via Benedetto Croce 46. No phone. $.*

2 ★★★ Cappella Sansevero.

There's a real sense of hushed awe as you enter the cold, marble mausoleum of the princes of Sangro di Sansevero, where visitors come to marvel over one of the most celebrated works of art in Naples, Giuseppe Sammartino's *Cristo Velato* or Veiled Christ (1753). In the mid-1700s, amateur scientist Prince Raimondo di Sangro revamped the chapel that had been built in 1590 by his ancestor, Giovan Francesco, employing a team of heavyweight artists and sculptors to decorate the interior. Sammartino was only 33 when he produced the masterpiece that stands in the middle of the chapel. The thin veil draped over Christ's prone body is so uncannily lifelike that you're tempted to reach out and smooth its soft folds. Among the other statues in the chapel, Francesco Quierolo's *Disillusion* (1753–54) is remarkable for the virtuosic fishing net draped over the standing male figure. The statue on the left of the altar is also worth a good look; *Veiled Modesty* is considered the masterpiece of Neapolitan sculptor Antonio Corradini (1668–1752). *See p 19,* **6**.

La Sfogliatella Mary.

3 ★★★ Pio Monte della Misericordia.

One of Naples' most important paintings is in this small, octagonal church, commissioned by a charitable institution of seven men whose aim was to alleviate the suffering of the poor through good works, illustrated in Caravaggio's *Seven Acts of Mercy* over the high altar. Painted in 1607, this dark, dramatic work, with its extraordinary chiaroscuro effects, shows the Virgin and Child borne by angels with huge wings in the context of an earthy street scene set in the Spaccanapoli. The small picture gallery (take the stairs or elevator in the courtyard to the second floor) contains works by Luca Giordano, Massimo Stazione, Giuseppe Ribera, and other Neapolitan painters from the 17th and 18th centuries. In the third room is the modest, 7-sided table where the original members of the institution met (the confraternity still exists today) while the Sala Coretto opens onto a secret gallery from which the governors could spy

Contemporary art lovers should head for the excellent MADRe museum.

into the church; it looks directly onto the painting. *See p 14,* ⑩.

④ ★ Pinacoteca Girolamini.

The first time I found myself in the Girolamini monastery complex just across the road from the Duomo, it was by accident; few tourists venture here and it's not included on many itineraries. However, I would strongly advise art lovers to pop in to see the small but rewarding pinacoteca housing some fine examples of Neapolitan 16th- to 18th-century painting. The entrance takes you through a serene white and gray cloister planted with orange and lemon

trees. Inside, there are only a handful of rooms but they contain works by heavyweights such as Massimo Stanzione, Giuseppe Ribera, Guido Reni, and Andrea Vaccaro. Look out for Caracciolo's *Baptism of Christ* (c. 1610) with its dramatic chiaroscuro effects and Ribera's Sant'Andrea (painted between 1610 and 1620) with amazingly lifelike skin on the saint's face and head. ⏱ *30 min. Via del Duomo 142.* ☎ *081/449139. Free admission. Mon–Sat 9:30am–12:50pm. Metro Cavour.*

⑤ ★★ MADRe. The inauguration of the **Museo d'Arte Contemporanea Donna Regina Napoli** in 2005 was part of several recent initiatives putting Naples on the contemporary culture map. Three floors of rooms house temporary exhibition spaces plus an impressive permanent collection of works by both internationally known names such as Anish Kapoor, Jeff Koons, Damien Hirst, and Rebecca Horn, and contemporary Italian artists such as Mimmo Paladino and Mario Schifano. ⏱ *45 min. Via Settembrini 79.* ☎ *081/5624561. www.museomadre.it. Admission 3.50€, free Mon. Mon, Wed, Thurs, Sun 10am–9pm, Fri, Sat 10am–midnight. Metro Cavour or Museo.*

Museo di Capodimonte.

The splendid ceiling of the Sala Capitolo, Certosa di San Martino.

⑥ MADRe Café. For a quick break, the museum café is the best bet in the area. At lunchtime, it serves pizza, sandwiches, and salads, and during the rest of the day you can order drinks and a cake. *Via Settembrini 79.* ☎ *081/19313016. $–$$.*

⑦ ★★ Certosa di San Martino. For art lovers, this Carthusian monastery complex contains many treasures. Start in the Certosa church where, among the marble intarsia and gilded stuccoes, there's an exemplary array of Neapolitan baroque painting. The rooms behind the altar, especially the Sala Capitolo, the Sala del Tesoro, and the Sacristy, have elaborate frescoed ceilings The **Museo dell'Opera** art gallery is laid out in rooms around the Great Cloister and includes a section devoted to images of Naples from the 1400s–1800s. Among the old maps and painted images of the city is the anonymous, 15th-century Tavola Strozzi showing monuments such as the Certosa and the Castel Sant'Elmo and a series of gruesome paintings of the plague epidemic of 1656. The sumptuous ex-prior's residence in the south wing features a series of extravagant, frescoed rooms where you can see paintings by such 17th and 18th-century masters as Stanzione, Lanfranco, and Ribera. Micco Spadaro painted the ceilings in Rooms 14 to 16, from where there are also fantastic views. See p 18, ❶.

⑧ ★★★ Museo di Capodimonte. There's no better place in southern Italy to look at Renaissance and baroque painting than here in the Bourbons' scarlet-painted ex-hunting lodge-cum-sumptuous palace. Hanging on the walls are works by Raphael, Masaccio, Botticelli, Simone Martini, Bellini, Titian, Caravaggio, and many, many more. See p 42 for full tour.

Detail of the ceiling frescoes in the Sala Capitolo, Certosa di San Martino.

Museo di Capodimonte

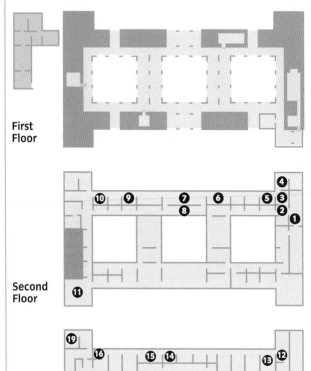

First Floor

Second Floor

Third Floor

1 Room 2	**7** Room 12	**13** Room 67
2 Room 3	**8** Rooms 13-14	**14** Room 74
3 Room 5	**9** Room 17	**15** Room 75
4 Room 6	**10** Room 19	**16** Room 78
5 Room 8	**11** Royal Apartments (Rooms 31-60)	**17** Room 87
6 Room 11	**12** Room 65	**18** Room 91
		19 Top Floor Galleries

This imposing red and gray building contains one of Italy's most important art museums, although it was originally Carlo III's hunting lodge, built in 1738. An inheritance from Carlo's mother, Elisabetta Farnese, together with the Borghese collection, makes up the core of what we see today. Paintings hang according to areas of origin and in chronological order. START: **Bus M4, M5 or 178 to the Museum. Trip length: three hours.**

Museo di Capodimonte, once a royal hunting lodge.

❶ ★★ Room 2. Rooms 2–30 make up the Farnese Gallery, where the haul of art amassed by several generations of the Farnese family from Parma hangs. In Room 2, Titian's c. 1545 portrait of Pope Paul III (Alessandro Farnese, founder of the family art collection) and his grandsons is a masterpiece. Raphael's portrait of Farnese shows him as a mere cardinal.

❷ ★★ Room 3. The Tuscan and Umbrian schools are showcased in the next rooms. Here, a small, glowing *Crucifixion* by Masaccio shows early signs of experimentation with perspective (a technique in which he was to become a master).

❸ ★★ Room 5. Two early altarpieces by Masolino hang here, the 1428 *Foundation of Santa Maria Maggiore* (with its architectural background) showing further

evidence of the new interest in perspective.

❹ ★★ Room 6. The *Virgin and Child with Angels* (1468–69) is an early work by Botticelli who, at the time, was still influenced by Filippo Lippi. Lippi's *Annunciation* (with Florence's Duomo in the background) hangs in the same room. There's also a *Madonna and Child* by Perugino.

❺ ★ Room 8. The focus switches to the Venetian school with Giovanni Bellini's exemplary *Transfiguration* (1480–85) showing typical experimentation with light and color.

❻ ★★★ Room 11. Titian's erotically charged *Danae* (c. 1544) shows the daughter of King Argos being seduced by Jupiter in the form of a shower of gold; the model was a famous courtesan, possibly mistress of Cardinal Alessandro Farnese in whose private rooms the painting hung. El Greco's *El Soplon* is based on a painting by the Ancient Greek artist Antiphilos and shows a wonderful play of light in the boy's illuminated face.

⑦ ★★★ Room 12. Works from Emilia Romagna include a favorite of mine, Parmigianino's portrait of the famous courtesan *Anthea* (1530–35), as well as Correggio's *Mystic Marriage of St. Catherine* (c. 1520).

⑧ ★ Rooms 13–14. Some of the Farnese's dazzling collection of 'curios' are housed here: small bronzes, majolica-ware, ivories, jewelry, coins, and glass.

⑨ ★ Room 17. Flemish painter Pieter Breughel makes a surprise appearance with several works, including the disturbing *Parable of the Blind Men* (1568).

⑩ ★ Room 19. This representation of the *Mystic Marriage of St. Catherine* was painted by Annibale Carracci in c. 1585.

⑪ ★★ Royal Apartments (Rooms 31–60). The sumptuous Royal Apartments include a Pompeian salon, the state ballroom done out in gold, and Queen Amelia's boudoir, entirely lined with Capodimonte porcelain panels.

⑫ ★★★ Room 65. Here you'll find 13th–19th-century works originating in Naples, including works by all the Neapolitan greats: Francesco Solimena, Massimo Stanzione, Giuseppe Ribera, and Luca Giordano. A highlight is Simone Martini's golden 1317 *St. Ludovico of Toulouse* from the church of San Lorenzo Maggiore that now hangs in its own darkened room. The painting was commissioned by Robert d'Anjou.

⑬ ★ Room 67. Colantonio's *Saint Jerome in his Study* (1445), complete with soft-eyed lion, also comes from San Lorenzo and was part of a two-tiered altarpiece.

⑭ ★ Room 74. Giorgio Vasari's *Presentation in the Temple* was painted for the church of Monteoliveto in Naples.

Royal Apartments, Capodimonte.

15 ★★ **Room 75.** Titian's great *Annunciation* (c. 1557) comes from San Domenico Maggiore. Look at that incredible shaft of light as the clouds open.

16 ★★★ **Room 78.** Caravaggio's dramatic *Flagellation* (1609–10) also hung in San Domenico Maggiore. This painting, with its extraordinary chiaroscuro effects, influenced generations of Neapolitan painters.

17 ★★ **Room 87.** Artemesia Gentileschi's gory, vengeful *Judith Beheading Holofernes* (c. 1618) shows the Jewish heroine killing the Assyrian general Holofernes in his sleep.

18 ★ **Room 91.** Ribera's pot-bellied *Drunken Silenus* (1626) shows Bacchus in full party mode surrounded by nymphs and satyrs.

19 ★ **Top Floor Galleries.** The top floor houses the section dedicated to 19th-century paintings, contemporary art (including Sol LeWitt's 2002 *White Bands in a Black Room*), photography, and temporary exhibitions. The most

Caravaggio's Flagellation.

famous work here is Andy Warhol's erupting *Vesuvius* (1985).

Practical Matters

The Museo di Capodimonte is at Via Miano 2 (☎ 081/7499111). Admission is 7.50€ adults, 6.50€ after 2pm; 3.50€ for E.U. citizens 18 to 25 yrs, free for E.U. citizens under 18 and over 65. It's open Thursday to Tuesday 8:30am to 7:30pm (last entry 6:30pm). Bus M4, M5, 178.

A Breath of Fresh Air

After all that art, you may feel the need for a breather, and luckily, Capodimonte boasts the vast **Bosco di Capodimonte,** a 130-hectare (320-acre) park laid out in 1742 by Fernando di Sanfelice to cater for Charles of Bourbon's passion for hunting. The area immediately surrounding the museum building is characterized by smooth lawns and neat pathways dotted with trees and shrubs. Being a rare Naples green space, it's crowded on weekends with families and teenagers kicking balls around, but for peace and quiet, walk just a hundred meters or so to the west and you find yourself in semi-deserted woodland, cut by shady walkways popular with joggers. Scattered among the woods are various crumbling buildings, such as the **Reale Fabbrica delle Porcellane,** the ex-Capodimonte porcelain factory (located to the south) dating from 1743. Nearby is the church of **San Gennaro,** founded by Charles of Bourbon in 1745.

Hidden Naples

CAPODIMONTE

Osservatorio Astronomico

MATERDEI

Materdei Ⓜ

Museo Archeologico Nazionale

Ⓜ Museo S. Gennaro

Galleria Principe di Napoli

Stazione Ⓕ ▣ Montesano

Ⓜ Dante

Castel Sant'Elmo

Certosa di S. Martino

QUARTIERI SPAGNOLI

Galleria Umberto I

Palazzo Reale

SANTA LUCIA

S. Chiara

Posta Centrale

Università di Napoli

Musei Scienze Naturali

CENTRO STORICO

Golfo di Napoli

Map legend

ⓘ	Information
✉	Post Office
Ⓜ	Metro

Scale: 0 – 1000 ft / 0 – 300 m

❶ Catacombe di San Gennaro
❷ Palazzo dello Spanuolo
❸ Orto Botanico
❹ San Giovanni a Carbonara
❺ Santa Maria Donnaregina Vecchia
❻ Il Pizzaiolo del Presidente
❼ Battistero di San Giovanni in Fonte
❽ Chiostro di San Gregorio Armeno
❾ Quartieri Spagnoli
❿ Galleria di Palazzo Zevallos Stigliano
⓫ La Caffettiera

Most visitors to Naples stick to the well-worn itineraries of must-sees, and leave without realizing that there's a lot more to the city than a (world-famous) archaeological museum and the Duomo. These are some of my favorite low-key places, guaranteed to provide an escape from the crowds. START: **Bus 24, 110, R4 to the Church of the Madonna del Buon Consiglio.**

① ★★ Catacombe di San Gennaro. Of all Naples' underground sights, I think these catacombs, burial place of the city's revered patron saint and the oldest Paleo-Christian burial ground in the city, are the most atmospheric and impressive. You can visit the huge chambers containing tombs topped with ancient mosaics and vaults carved out of the ground and the tufa walls. See p 55, **⑨**.

② ★ Palazzo dello Spanuolo. This pale green and cream baroque confection is my favorite building in Naples. Ferdinando Sanfelice (1675–1748) was the greatest of all Neapolitan baroque architects and a trademark feature was the double external 'flying' staircase, of which the beautifully restored Palazzo dello Spanuolo has the most impressive example. It lies in the once-elegant but now very scruffy Sanità neighborhood; buildings such as this palazzo hint at another world. It's closed to the public, but you can admire the exterior from the courtyard. ⏲ *10 min. Via dei Vergini 19. Metro Piazza Cavour.*

③ ★★ kids Orto Botanico. In a city where green space is at a premium, this botanical garden is a delight. The thundering traffic of Via Foria seems worlds away as you walk among the beautifully maintained paths and examples of plant and tree species from all over the world. Take your time to explore. *Via Foria 223.* ☎ *081/449759.* ⏲ *45 min. www.ortobotanico.unina.it. Free admission, but call ahead. Mon–Fri 9am–2pm. Metro Piazza Cavour. See also p 68.*

④ ★★★ San Giovanni a Carbonara. Another personal favorite, this church has superb Renaissance sculptures and the round, frescoed Ser Caracciolo del Sole chapel with its lovely old majolica floor. The

Palazzo dello Spanuolo's magnificent flying staircase.

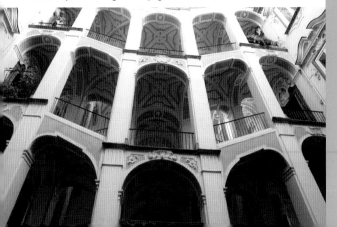

15th-century frescoes vividly illustrate the lives of hermits; the panels on the right of the door are particularly charming. *See p 33,* ❶.

❺ ★★ **Santa Maria Donnaregina Vecchia.** For years, this church was closed to visitors unless you had an appointment; now it's part of the MADRe contemporary art museum, and is open to all. Visitors rarely bother with a stop here, but I urge you not to miss it for Tino da Camaino's tomb of Queen Mary of Hungary and the 14th-century frescoes by Pietro Cavallino. *See p 33,* ❷.

❻ ★★ **Il Pizzaiolo del Presidente.** Pizza makes a good, quick lunch break and Il Presidente makes one of the best; Bill Clinton (one-time customer) thought so too. Eat in or take out, and go for a simple pizza Margherita. *Via dei Tribunale 120.* ☎ *081/210903. $.*

❼ ★★ **Battistero di San Giovanni in Fonte.** Accessed through the Duomo, the Baptistery of San Giovanni in Fonte, dating from the 4th to 5th century, is the oldest building of its kind in the Western world and has a dazzling mosaic in its dome. ⏱ *10 min. For the Duomo, see p 14,* ⓫. *Archaeological area and Baptistery: Admission 3€. Mon–Sat 9am–noon, 4:30–6:30pm.*

❽ ★★★ **Chiostro di San Gregorio Armeno.** My favorite cloister in Naples is a peaceful haven in the heart of the crazy *centro storico*. The entrance is through an iron gate and at the top of a long staircase; as you pass through the carved wood doors, notice the old bronze revolving drums on either side through which supplies were passed to the nuns. The cloister, enclosed by the weathered old ochre walls of the convent and planted with orange trees, is a sunny space filled with birdsong. ⏱ *15 min. Via Maffei 1.* ☎ *081/*

The peaceful cloister of San Gregorio Armeno.

5520186. Voluntary donation. Mon–Fri 9:30am–noon, Sat & Sun 9:30am–1pm. Metro Dante or Montesanto.

❾ ★ Quartieri Spagnoli. It's a shame that this neighborhood of tight-knit streets has such an exaggerated reputation as a hotbed of crime, because it's a slice of true Naples, warts and all. The cramped area was built to house occupying Spanish troops in the 16th century and subsequently became one of the city's most poverty stricken districts. It still suffers from many problems today, but for the tourist, it's a colorful area of tiny shops, neighborhood bars and *osterie*, shabby streets lined with laundry hanging out to dry, and modest, crowded dwellings. Do not, however, venture into this area after dark and in the dead period during the afternoon siesta; and do keep bags and cameras close. 🕐 *30 min. To the west of Via Toldeo, between Piazza Trieste e Trento and Piazza Carità. Metro Dante or Montesanto.*

❿ Galleria di Palazzo Zevallos Stigliano. The magnificent headquarters of the Banca Intesa hides one masterpiece among its small collection of paintings. Take the elevator to the second floor to see Caravaggio's 1610 *Martyrdom of Sant'Ursula,* which hangs in its own room. It was graceing the bank manager's office until 2007. 🕐 *15 min.*

Space is tight in the Quartieri Spagnoli.

Via Toledo 185. ☎ *800/088622. www.palazzozevallos.com. Admission 3€. Mon–Sat 10am–6pm. Metro Dante or funicolare (funicular) to Montesanto.*

⓫ ★ La Caffettiera. A 10-minute walk along Via Chiaia brings you to lovely Piazza dei Martiri and this fine old bar whose elegant terrace makes an ideal spot for a cocktail. *Piazza dei Martiri 30.* ☎ *081/7644243. $–$$.*

Naples' Secret Places

If you're lucky enough to be in Naples between the last weekend in April and the first in June, you can catch the Maggio dei Monumenti ('Monuments in May') festival, which presents a unique opportunity to explore some of the city's otherwise closed palazzi, gardens, churches, and other sites. A program of guided tours and visits plus concerts and exhibitions focuses on some of Naples' most inaccessible gems. Information can be difficult to find, but the best place to start is the tourist office (see 'Savvy Traveler,' p 163).

Underground Naples

1. Duomo: Area Archeologico
2. Scavi di San Lorenzo
3. Napoli Sotterranea
4. Timpani e Tempura
5. Santa Chiara
6. Stazioni dell'Arte (starting at Piazza Dante)
7. Gelateria Otranto
8. Catacombe di San Gaudioso
9. Catacombe di San Gennaro

0	1000 ft
0	300 m

i Information

✉ Post Office

Ⓜ Metro

FONTANELLE

MATERDEI

ARENELLA

VOMERO

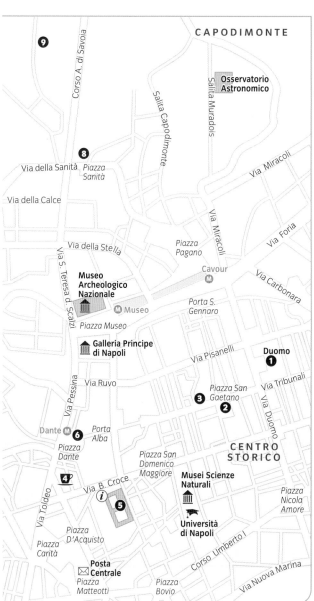

CAPODIMONTE

Corso A. di Savoia

Osservatorio Astronomico

Salita Muradois

Salita Capodimonte

Via Miracoli

Via della Sanità   *Piazza Sanità*

Via Foria

Via della Calce

Via della Stella

Via S. Teresa d. Scalzi

Via Miracoli

Piazza Pagano

Cavour Ⓜ

Via Carbonara

Museo Archeologico Nazionale

Ⓜ Museo

Porta S. Gennaro

Piazza Museo

Galleria Principe di Napoli

Via Pisanelli

Duomo ❶

Via Ruvo

Via Pessina

❸ *Piazza San Gaetano* ❷

Via Tribunali

Via Duomo

Dante Ⓜ❻

Porta Alba

Piazza Dante

Piazza San Domenico Maggiore

CENTRO STORICO

🀫 ❹

Via B. Croce

ⓘ

❺

Musei Scienze Naturali

Piazza Nicola Amore

Università di Napoli

Via Toledo

Piazza D'Acquisto

Corso Umberto I

Piazza Carità

Posta Centrale

Piazza Matteotti

Piazza Bovio

Via Nuova Marina

There's a lot more to Naples than meets the eye; quite literally. Evidence of its multilayered history and past inhabitants is buried under modern-day street level. The following itinerary provides real insight into the city's distant (and no so distant) past.
START: **Metro Cavour to the Duomo.**

① ★ Duomo: Area Archeologico. The early Christian basilica of Santa Restituta (now part of the Duomo) was built in the 4th century on the site of a temple to Apollo and offers access to a small but interesting archaeological site. Steps to the left of Santa Restituta's apse lead underground to a complex of buildings that date from the Greek period through the Romans to the Dark Ages. It's a bit confusing and not well labeled, but you can see the remains of a Roman portico and a street with indentations made by cartwheels plus an open area with fragments of mosaic paving dating from the 5th century A.D. See also p 34, ⑩. ⏲ *30 min. Admission 3€. Mon–Sat 9am–noon, 4:30–6:30pm. Metro Cavour.*

② ★★★ kids Scavi di San Lorenzo. The totally fascinating

archaeological area below the church of San Lorenzo (entrance through the far right-hand corner of the cloister) reveals a subterranean world on different levels, spanning several centuries. Here stood ancient Neapolis's business zone, which included the Greek *agora* (assembly place) and the Roman forum as well as a complex comprising a *macellum* (food market) and other shops. Work is ongoing, but so far an almost intact, 2,000-year old *cardo* (street) has been revealed on which stands a butcher shop, a laundry, and a graceful brick arcade. ⏲ *40 min. Via dei Tribunali 316.* ☎ *081/2110860. www.sanlorenzo maggiorenapoli.it. Admission 5€. Mon–Sat 9am–5pm, Sun 9:30am–1pm. Metro Dante.*

③ ★★★ kids Napoli Sotteranea. Not for the claustrophobic,

Going underground at the Duomo.

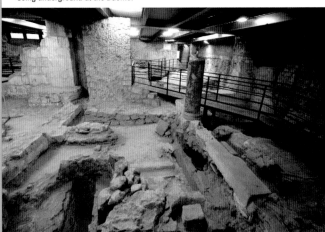

Napoli Sotteranea.

Underground Naples is a fascinating tour revealing the layers of history that lie beneath the modern city by way of a maze of tunnels, aqueducts, and chambers. The earliest of these excavations is believed to date from 5,000 years ago. The ancient Greeks quarried for tufa stone to build their walls and temples and the Romans built a large aqueduct and a series of underground walkways. In the early 1600s, a new aqueduct was added to the complex water system, but this was abandoned in the early 1900s by which time the underground maze of tunnels totaled around 270 miles in length. During World War II, tracts of the tunnels and caverns were reopened and used as bomb shelters. The excellent guided tour (also in English) leads you through sections of this underground labyrinth, recounting its story as you go. ⏰ 1½ hr. *Piazza San Gaetano 68.* 📞 *081/296944. www.napolisotteranea.org. Admission 9:30€ adults, 8€ students, 6€ under-12s, free under-5s. Tours every 2 hr. Mon–Fri noon–4pm, Sat & Sun 10am–6pm. Metro Dante.*

4 ★★ **Timpani e Tempura.** This little place serves a delicious modern take on traditional Neapolitan street food, which you can eat in or take away: baked rice sartù, pasta timbale, deep-fried veg, and pâté and savory mousses. *Vico della Quercia 17.* 📞 *081/5512280. $.*

5 ★ **Santa Chiara.** The small archaeological area of Santa Chiara is included in the ticket to the museum adjacent to the church. It reveals a Roman spa complex dating from the late 1st century A.D. comprising a pool with intact benches and access stairs, a gym, a *laconicum* (a type of ancient sauna), a *tepidarium* (for warm water bathing), and what is believed to be the *frigidarium* (for cold water bathing). *See p 13,* **7**.

6 ★★ **kids** **Stazioni dell'Arte.** Naples' growing reputation as a showcase for contemporary art spreads as far as its metro stations, some of which are home to an eclectic series of installations by local artists and internationally known names. The modest price of

The Materdei metro stop.

the train ticket makes it one of the cheapest shows in town. Most of the stations involved are on Line 1, between Piazza Dante and Vanvitelli. The ticket is valid for 90 minutes, so it's possible to start at one end, hop off at each stop, and take the train back to your starting point. Remember that the installations are mounted on various levels of the stations, so use the escalators, and explore. Works to look out for include Jannis Kounellis's untitled train tracks and squashed shoes (Piazza Dante), Sol LeWitt's Wall Drawings (Materdei), Perino & Vele's life-sized Fiat 500s (Salvatore Rosa), mosaics by Isabelle Ducrot, and Mario Merz's light installation (Vanvitelli). 🕐 *1 hr; avoid rush hour 7:30– 9:30am and 6–8pm.* ☎ *800/568866. www.metro.na.it. Train tickets 1.10€, valid 90 min. Daily 6:30am– 11pm. Metro Dante or Vanvitelli.*

7 ★★ **Gelateria Otranto.** Hop off the metro at Vanvitelli in Vomero and head for this gelateria that, according to many locals, makes the best ice cream in town. The fresh fruit flavors are fantastic, but the chestnut and rum or pear and ricotta are also mouth-watering. *Via Scarlatti 78.* ☎ *081/5587498. $.*

8 ★★ **Catacombe di San Gaudioso.** These catacombs were dug in Roman times as water cisterns, and first used as burial chambers in the 5th century. St Gaudiosus, an African bishop, was buried here in 452 and the practice continued until 1660. The entrance is through the church of Santa Maria della Sanità. A fascinating guided tour leads through a series of chambers at different levels revealing early mosaic and fresco fragments as well as various bizarre burial techniques. In one method, used in the mid-17th century, the corpse was placed in a sitting position, the head secured to the wall with cement. Once drained of fluids, the skull and body were removed separately; the body was buried and the skull was placed over a frescoed image of the deceased. You can see traces of these portraits complete with head niche. Other bodies were placed in a fetal position in long niches carved out of the soft tufa walls.

Claustrophobics might find these catacombs difficult; those at San Gennaro (see **9**) are more spacious. 🕐 *30 min. Via della Sanita 124.* ☎ *081/5441305. www. santamariadellasanita.it. Admission 5€ adults, 3€ 5–16 yrs. Tours daily every 45 min. 9:30am–12:30pm. Metro Piazza Cavour or Museo.*

Cimitero delle Fontanelle

Consisting of a huge cavern, this ex-quarry was first used as a burial site in the 17th century and played a significant role in the 1835 cholera epidemic, when all Naples' dead were moved here from the city's other cemeteries. This process was repeated in the 1974 outbreak and some 40,000 skulls and bones were eventually piled high in the enormous space. That's what you see today; piles and piles of bones. It's an awe-inspiring sight. Call the tourist office (☎ 081/402394) about visiting.

⑨ ★★ Catacombe di San Gennaro. These two-level catacombs cover a huge area and were also used as burial places (unlike those in Rome, which were hideouts for persecuted Christians). Believed to date from the 2nd century, the catacombs became an important place of pilgrimage by the 5th century after the body of San Gennaro was brought here from Pozzuoli (p 47, ❶). The guided tour starts on the upper level in a series of spacious, open chambers where you can see different types of tombs:

locoli of different sizes hewn out of the walls (the smallest were for babies) and others in the floor. Important families were given their own side chapel wherein the walls were decorated with frescoes, a few of which survive. On the lower level (where excavations are still in progress), you can see the remains of an early basilica and an 8th-century baptismal font. ⏱ *40 min. Via Capodimonte 16.* ☎ *081/7411071. Admission 5€ adults, 3€ 5–16 yrs. Tours Tues–Sun 9am, 10am, 11am, noon, 2pm, & 3pm. Bus R4.*

Tombs at the San Gennaro catacombs.

Naples with **Kids**

1. Pintauro
2. Sightseeing Buses
3. Christmas Cribs
4. Ospedale delle Bambole
5. Disney Store
6. Antiche Delizie
7. Villa Comunale
8. Aquarium
9. Certosa di San Martino

Parco di Capodimonte

Tondo di Capodimonte

Museo di Capodimonte

CAPODIMONTE

Salita Di Mauro

Corso A. di Savoia

Salita Capodimonte

Salita Muradois

Via Miracoli

MATERDEI

Via della Calce

Piazza Sanità

Piazza Pagano

Via Foria

ARENELLA

Piazza De Leva

Via M. R. Via Imbriani

Materdei

Via S. Rosa

Via Pontecorvo

Museo Archeologico Nazionale

Cavour

Porta S. Gennaro

Piazza Musil Medaglie d'Oro

Salvator Rosa Via S. Rosa

Museo Piazza Museo

Via Pessina

Via Ruvo

Duomo

Piazza Medaglie d'Oro

Piazza Leonardo

Stazione Montesano

Dante

Piazza San Gaetano

Piazza Fanzago

Via Bernini

Piazza Dante

Via B. Croce

CENTRO STORICO

Via Duomo

VOMERO

Via T. Angelini

Piazza Montesanto

Via Scura

S. Chiara

Corso Umberto I

Vanvitelli

Castel Sant'Elmo

Piazza Carità

Posta Centrale

Piazza Matteotti

Piazza Bovio

Via Depretis

Via C. Colombo

CHIAIA

QUARTIERI SPAGNOLI

Via Toledo

Bacino del Piliero

Piazza Amedeo

V. d. Mille

Galleria Umberto I

Piazza Municipio

Castel Nuovo

Stazione Marittima

Villa Pignatelli

Via Chiaia

Piazza d. Martiri

Piazza del Plebiscito

Palazzo Reale

Via Acton

Molo Beverello

Riviera di Chiaia

SANTA LUCIA

Via S. Lucia

Via N. Sauro

Piazza Vittoria

Villa Comunale

V. Partenope

Golfo di Napoli

Castel d'Ovo

	Information
✉	Post Office
Ⓜ	Metro

0 — 2000 ft
0 — 600 m

Although Naples doesn't have many specifically child-oriented attractions, like the rest of Italy, it's bambino-friendly. Here are some suggestions about how to keep the little ones amused when the city's museums and churches become too much. If all else fails, there's always pizza and gelato. START: **Bus 24, C22, C57 to the southern end of Via Toledo.**

1 ★★ **Pintauro.** This hole-in-the-wall pastry shop may be lacking in frills, but it serves perhaps the best sfogliatelle in town; the babà (yeast cakes) are good too. Eat your breakfast standing at the marble counter with the locals. *Via Toledo 275.* ☎ *081/417339. $.*

2 ★★ **Sightseeing Buses.** Naples' hop-on hop-off open-topped tourist buses cover the whole city in four interchangeable routes, which extend as far as Capodimonte, Capo Posillipo, and all the way out to Vesuvius. It's a fun way to move around, and views from the upper deck are splendid. Many of the places suggested on this tour are accessible from the tour bus stops. ⏱ *2 hr. minimum. Info and terminal Largo Castello/Piazza Municipio.* ☎ *081/5517279. www.napoli.city-sightseeing.it. Tickets 22€ adults, 11€ 6–15 yrs, 66€ family ticket (2 adults and 2 under-18s). Hours vary between the routes, but buses leave roughly 10am–5pm daily.*

3 ★★★ **Christmas Cribs.** Most Neapolitan families set up a Christmas crib at home. These can be huge, involving dozens (even hundreds) of figures, some with moving parts, set in elaborate rural landscapes complete with lighting effects. Neapolitan craftspeople have been making these *presepi* for centuries and many of the workshops are located in and around Via San Gregorio Armeni. In the run up to Christmas, the street is

Christmas cribs.

jam-packed. ⏱ *40 min. Via San Gregorio Armeni. Metro Dante.*

4 ★ **Ospedale delle Bambole.** Even if you don't have a sick doll to be treated, it's fun to go along and have a look at this famous Doll's Hospital, which is stuffed to overflowing with every kind of doll imaginable (many of them really old) and all sorts of doll body parts. ⏱ *30 min. Via S. Biagio dei Librai 81.* ☎ *081/203067. www.ospedaledelle bambole.it. Free admission. Mon–Sat 9am–1pm. Metro Dante.*

5 ★ **kids Disney Store.** Kids can only take so much art and culture, pizza, and gelato, but help is on hand at the Naples branch of the Disney Store, which is stocked with all the usual Disney paraphernalia.

To the Beach

Thanks to the poor water quality in the sea immediately surrounding Naples, you have to head out toward Posillipo for reasonably clean swimming, although the beaches here are small and shingly. One of the best is at **Ponticello a Marechiaro** where you can rent deck chairs and umbrellas in season. Take the C23 bus from Posillipo, get off in the little piazzetta where all the restaurants are, and take the path round to the right down to the sea. For proper, sandy beaches, go to the island of **Procida** for the day (see p 158); the boat ride is fun too.

🕐 30 min. Via Toledo 129. ☎ 081/ 7901377. Free admission. Mon–Sat 10am–8pm, Sun 10am–2pm, 4.40– 8pm. Metro Dante or Montesanto.

6 ★ **Antiche Delizie.** I suggest a lunchtime picnic in the Villa Comunale park (see **7**). Call in at this little deli to stock up on picnic food; you can buy the ingredients to make up a sandwich or a homemade dish to go. *Via Pasquale Scura 14.* ☎ *081/5513088. $.*

7 ★★ **Villa Comunale.** Despite the nearby traffic, this public park is quite peaceful and is a safe run-around space for youngsters. There's no grass but lots of benches on which to enjoy a picnic. There's also a splendid 1887 bandstand, the oldest aquarium in Europe (see **8**), a children's playground, and a café. At the eastern end are rides for toddlers; mini-pony drawn carts, electric cars, and bicycle carriages for a gentle peddle around the park. 🕐 *1 hr. Riviera di Chiaia. No phone. Free*

Doll's hospital.

Out of Town Kids' Stuff

Two of Naples' best attractions for youngsters are located **some** way from the city center. The excellent **Città delle Scienze** (☎ 081/7352111; www.cittadellescienze.it; admission 7€ adults, 5€ 3–18 yr olds; Planetarium ticket 2€) is housed in an ex-industrial building in Bagnoli and is crammed with interactive exhibits that, through a very hands-on approach, address all aspects of science. Take the Metro to Bagnoli, and then Bus C1 or 129. The **Edenlandia funfair** (☎ 081/239409; www.edenlandia.it; admission 2.50€, each ride 2€; admission including unlimited rides 10€; free admission for kids under 1.10m (3.66 ft) in height) is in the suburb of Fuorigrotta; catch the Cumana rail to Edenlandia. Rides include a big dipper, dodgems, a Chinese dragon, a Tower, a ghost train, and a section with safe rides for tinies. There's also a 3-D cinema and several bars and restaurants.

Science City; a great place for curious kids.

admission. May–Oct daily 7am–midnight, Nov–Apr daily 7am–10pm. Bus 140, 152, C28, C4, R3.

8 ★★ **Aquarium.** Opened in 1874, Europe's first public aquarium maintains its original layout with a series of old-fashioned tanks containing sea creatures from local waters including huge, evil-looking moray eels, sea turtles, sea horses, and a writhing octopus. ⏱ *30 min. Villa Comunale, Riviera di Chiaia.* ☎ *081/5833111. Admission 1.50€. Nov–Feb Tues–Sat 9am–5pm, Sun 9am–2pm, Mar–Oct Tues–Sat 9am–6pm, Sun 9:30am–7:30pm. Bus 140, 152, C28, C4, R3.*

9 ★★ **Certosa di San Martino.** A couple of sections here are interesting for younger visitors. The collection of 18th-century nativity scenes ranges from tiny examples in glass cases to the famous *presepe Cuciniello*, which takes up most of the room. The tiniest crib is in Room 3; it's constructed in an eggshell. Among the displays are examples of the typical wood and terracotta figures with amazing detailing and of crib accessories (tiny plates of food, musical instruments, gifts, animals, and so on).

Kids will also enjoy the new **Sezione Navale,** or Maritime Museum, which houses a collection of model ships and ships' instruments including the full-sized Great Barge used by King Charles of Bourbon in the 1700s and King Umberto I of Savoy's white and gold barge with an eagle on the prow. *See p 18,* **1**.

Decumani

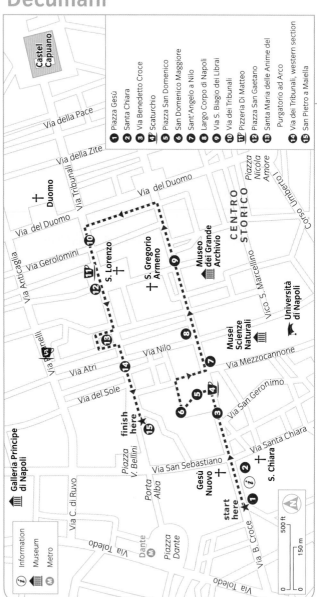

1. Piazza Gesù
2. Santa Chiara
3. Via Benedetto Croce
4. Scaturchio
5. Piazza San Domenico
6. San Domenico Maggiore
7. Sant'Angelo a Nilo
8. Largo Corpo di Napoli
9. Via S. Biagio dei Librai
10. Via dei Tribunali
11. Pizzeria Di Matteo
12. Piazza San Gaetano
13. Santa Maria delle Anime del Purgatorio ad Arco
14. Via dei Tribunali, western section
15. San Pietro a Maiella

This walk leads around the streets of the *centro storico,* which are still laid out on their Greco-Roman grid plan. Many of the city's key sights lie within this grid of ancient streets. Three main roads—the *decumani*—run east to west, intersected by narrower, north-south *cardines.* The principal street is the *decumanus inferior*, known as the Spaccanapoli. Via dei Tribunali (the *decumanus maior*) runs parallel to the north. START: **Metro Dante to Piazza Gesù. Walk length: two hours.**

Ever-colorful Spaccanapoli.

1 ★ **Piazza Gesù.** Start under the Guglia dell'Immacolata in the middle of the square. Built in 1747–50, this is one of the city's three towering rococo obelisks. The great rough-hewn façade on the western side of the square is of the church of Gésu Nuovo (see p 12, **6**).

2 ★★★ **Santa Chiara.** Walking east down Via Benedetto Croce, the solid, square tower straight ahead is the truncated campanile of the church of Santa Chiara (see p 13, **7**). Hidden within the convent complex is one of the loveliest cloisters in the city.

3 ★★★ **Via Benedetto Croce.** Lying at the heart of ancient Neapolis, the *decumanus inferior* teams with life at just about any time of day. Cross Via San Sebastiano (famous for its musical instrument

shops) and on the left at no.12 is 14th-century **Palazzo Filomarino,** its porticoed courtyard in better condition than most around here. In the courtyard of 18th-century **Palazzo Tufarelli** (no. 23) is an external 'flying staircase,' a feature of Neapolitan buildings of the time. You can see another at Palazzo Carafa della Spina (no. 45), but it's badly rundown.

4 ★★ **Scaturchio.** The ricotta-filled *sfogliatelle* pastries here are among the best in town and the alfresco terrace on the square is great if you have time to sit down. *Piazza San Domenico Maggiore 19.* ☎ *081/5516944. $.*

5 ★★ **Piazza San Domenico.** This lively square, with its ochre-hued

Spaccanapoli splits the old city in two.

palazzi and pavement cafés is a meeting place for locals, students, and tourists. The *guglia* (spire) was started in 1658 as thanks for deliverance from the plague. At no. 9 stands the imposing 16th-century **Palazzo Sangro** where madrigal composer Carlo Gesualdo (1566–1613) murdered his first wife Maria d'Avalos after finding her *in flagrante delicto* with her lover; after butchering them, he left their bodies in the piazza for all to see.

⑥ San Domenico Maggiore. The double flight of steps leading up from the square brings you in beside the high altar of this huge church, with its origins in the 13th century. Look out for the 14th-century frescoes by Roman artist Pietro Cavallino in the second side chapel on the right. *Piazza San Domenico Maggiore.* ☎ *081/459298. Free admission. Daily 8:30am–noon, 4:30–7pm.*

⑦ ★ Sant'Angelo a Nilo. With a striking dark red and gray façade, this church houses Florentine sculptor Donatello's only work in Naples,

a bas-relief of the *Assumption* on the tomb of Cardinal Brancaccio. *Piazzetta Nilo* ☎ *081/4201222. Free admission. Mon–Sat 9am–1pm, 4–6pm, Sun 9am–1pm.*

⑧ Largo Corpo di Napoli. Opposite the church is a famous Roman statue of the reclining Egyptian river god Nile, once an object of worship for the Egyptian community who inhabited the area. A rather earthier shrine hangs on the wall of the bar just ahead on the right; it's dedicated to Argentine soccer star Diego Maradona who, in the late 1980s, played for Napoli, the local football team.

⑨ ★★ Via S. Biagio dei Librai. Spaccanapoli eventually becomes Via S. Biagio dei Librai. The church of **San Nicola al Nilo** stands on the left; its pretty double staircase often shelters a few bric-a-brac stalls. Many of the shops along this stretch are dedicated to religious items: statues, vestments, chalices, and crosses in every form and size. On the right, at no. 114, is the entrance to the **Monte di Pietà chapel,** a prime example of baroque opulence. On the left, Via San Gregorio Armeno, famous for its Christmas cribs (see p 20, **⑩**), climbs the hill; the unusual bell tower straddling the road belongs to the church of San Gregorio. Up ahead at no. 81 is the Ospedale delle Bambole, a charming Doll's Hospital (p 57, **④**).

⑩ ★★ Via dei Tribunali. Turn left onto Via Duomo and left again onto the *Decumanus maior*, today's Via dei Tribunali. Often blocked by hooting cars and scooters, it's another lively street lined with small shops, grocery stalls, and crumbling palazzi. Immediately on your right is Il Pizzaiolo del Presidente (www. ilpizzaiolodelpresidente.it) which served pizza to Bill Clinton; the photo proves it. The road opens out onto Piazza Girolamini with its vast, white-fronted 17th-century church.

17 ★★ **Pizzeria Di Matteo.** It may be short on atmosphere, but this takeout eatery serves fantastic pizza (also in a deep-fried version), baked in the mosaic oven in the corner. Bill Clinton apparently ate here, too. *Via dei Tribunali 94.* ☎ *081/455262. $.*

12 ★ **Piazza San Gaetano.** Up ahead, Piazza San Gaetano lies on the site of the ancient Greek agorà and the Roman forum. The towering statue is of the saint himself; his halo lights up at night. On the left is the church of San Lorenzo (see p 21, **11**), on the right is the vast bulk of San Paolo and just beyond this is the entrance to the underground itinerary of Napoli Sotteranea (see p 52, **3**).

13 **Santa Maria delle Anime del Purgatorio ad Arco.** Farther along on the right is the church of Santa Maria del Purgatorio ad Arco, its railings topped by bronze skulls (see p 20, **7**).

14 ★ **Via dei Tribunali, western section.** At no. 33 (on the right) is a traditional water seller's booth, a throwback to the days when many residents of this area lacked fresh drinking water in their homes and had to buy it. Past this on the left is 18th-century **Palazzo Spinelli** with a grand courtyard and a splendid double staircase.

15 ★ **San Pietro a Maiella.** The tall, pointed bell tower ahead belongs to the 14th-century church of San Pietro a Maiella, a large monastery complex partly occupied by the Music Conservatory. Pop into the entrance on the left (no. 35) for a look at the cloister to a background of students practicing their scales. The Gothic church has an elaborate coffered ceiling. *Via dei Tribunali 39.* ☎ *081/459008. Free admission. Mon–Sat 7:30am–noon, 5:30–7pm, Sun 8:30am–1pm.*

Piazza San Domenico.

The Waterfront & Royal Naples

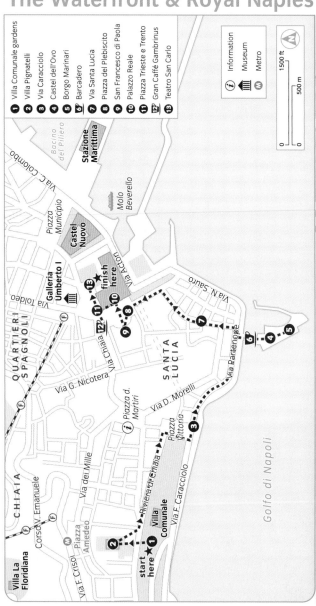

1 Villa Comunale gardens
2 Villa Pignatelli
3 Via Caracciolo
4 Castel dell'Ovo
5 Borgo Marinari
6 Barcadero
7 Via Santa Lucia
8 Piazza del Plebiscito
9 San Francesco di Paola
10 Palazzo Reale
11 Piazza Trieste e Trento
12 Gran Caffè Gambrinus
13 Teatro San Carlo

i Information
▥ Museum
Ⓜ Metro

This walk starts on the sunny waterfront, or *lungomare*, at the western end of the Villa Comunale gardens, near Piazza della Repubblica. This is a classic venue for Neapolitans, who come here to jog, walk their dogs, or stroll in the sun. It winds up at the San Carlo Opera House. START: **Bus 140, 152, C28, C4, or R3 to Villa Comunale gardens. Walk length: two hours.**

1 ★★ kids Villa Comunale gardens. The long, narrow park that runs parallel to the Chiaia seafront is surprisingly pleasant given the constant traffic that swirls around it. Laid out in 1781 as a royal garden, it was only open to the public on one day of the year. The elaborate glass and wrought iron bandstand in the middle dates from 1887. Nearby is a small Aquarium (see p 58, **8**), the oldest in Europe, dating from 1874. On sunny days, the park fills with families enjoying the fresh air. *See p 58,* **7**.

2 ★ Villa Pignatelli. Located on the northern side of the park is this neoclassical villa standing in an English-style garden. It was built in 1826 for Ferdinand Richard Acton, and passed through the hands of the Rothchild and Pignatelli families before being donated to the state in 1952, along with its precious contents of furniture, paintings, porcelain, and silver. *Riviera di Chiaia 200.* ☎ *081/669675. 2€. Wed–Mon 8:30am–2pm.*

3 ★★ Via Caracciolo. Cross over the park to Via Caracciolo (otherwise known as the *lungomare*) and head toward the Castel dell'Ovo with Capri on your right. On the left are a string of trendy waterfront restaurants and bars followed, as Via Caracciolo becomes Via Partenope, by a row of the city's classiest hotels, once setting for the Dolce Vita lifestyle of the world's glitterati.

4 ★ kids Castel dell'Ovo. On this tiny island of Megaris, the original Greek settlement of Paleopolis was founded around 680 B.C. Local legend says that when Virgil stayed on the site of the castle in the 1st century B.C, he buried an egg (*uovo*) claiming that when the egg broke, disaster would befall the city. Sitting on the rocky outcrop that juts into

Fishing boats and yachts share the moorings at Borgo Marinari.

the bay, the present-day castle was built by the Aragonese in the 16th century and is joined to the mainland by a solid bridge that's a popular spot for wedding photos. The castle is open for temporary exhibitions only, but you can walk around its terraces and ramparts from where there are splendid views of the bay. *Via Partenope.* ☎ *081/2400055. Free admission to terraces and ramparts. Mon–Sat 8am–sunset, Sun 8am–2pm.*

5 ★★ **Borgo Marinari.** This picturesque clutch of fishermen's cottages was saved from the extensive urban replanning that took place after the cholera epidemic of 1884. Sharing the tiny island of Megaris with the castle, it is a popular hangout for sultry summer evenings when the many restaurants and bars spill out onto the waterfront. Sunsets viewed from here are spectacular.

6 ★ **Barcadero.** A great spot for a light lunch or a drink, alfresco Barcadero has a terrace overlooking the marina beneath the Castel dell'Ovo bridge. The menu offers good sandwiches, salads, and other cold dishes. *Via Partenope (opposite the Castel dell'Ovo). No phone. Closed in bad weather. $–$$.*

7 **Via Santa Lucia.** Leave the seafront behind you and turn left up Via Santa Lucia. **Monte Echia,** the remains of a volcanic crater and part of ancient Paleopolis, rises up on your left. Roman general Lucullus built a vast villa at the top in the 1st century B.C. Borgo Santa Lucia was the old fishermen's quarter, full of narrow, cottage-lined streets that climb up the hill. Nowadays it's a picturesque neighborhood with lots of bars and restaurants.

8 ★ **Piazza del Plebiscito.** At the top of Via Santa Lucia, turn left. As you walk into wide-open Piazza del Plebiscito, notice the statues placed in the niches on the right; these are Kings of Naples, added to the Palazzo Reale in the late 1800s by Umberto I. This is one of Italy's most impressive squares, flanked by the massive Royal Palace and the church of San Francesco di Paola

Del Plebiscito and the church of San Francesco di Paola.

Palazzo Reale, a royal residence.

(see ⑨) and its sweeping double curve of graceful Doric columns. The equestrian statues of the two Bourbon kings, Charles III and Ferdinand I, are by Antonio Canova (1757–1822).

⑨ **San Francesco di Paola.** Bearing more than a passing resemblance to Rome's Pantheon (although the dome is 10 meters higher), the neoclassical church of San Francesco di Paola was built by King Ferdinand I in 1817. Impressive it may be, but the cool, gray and white marble interior is rather soulless. *Piazza del Plebiscito. No phone. Free admission. Mon–Sat 7:30am–noon, Sun 8:30am–12:30pm.*

⑩ ★★ **Palazzo Reale.** The Spanish Viceroy commissioned Domenico Fontana to build this splendid royal palace in 1600, but it has been enlarged and modified over the years. Inside, you can visit the lavish Royal Apartments, which include the ornate theater and the Palatine Chapel. It's worth going in just to see the double staircase. *See p 11,* ②.

⑪ **Piazza Trieste e Trento.** This square always seems to be teeming with a mix of locals and tourists, kids, pigeons, cars, and stray dogs. On the right is the church of **San Ferdinando** (1622) and nearby, an *acquafrescaia* booth where, in the old days, people who had no clean running water in their homes could buy drinking water.

⑫ ★★ **Gran Caffè Gambrinus.** The terrace of this old Art Deco café fills up in the early evening with locals and tourists enjoying a pre-dinner aperitivo. Try a Negroni, a lethal but delicious mix of gin, Martini Rosso and Campari. *Via Chiaia 1–2.* ☎ *081/417582. $–$$.*

⑬ ★★★ **Teatro San Carlo.** This glorious opera house was originally built in 1737 by Charles III of Bourbon, but reconstructed after a devastating fire in 1816. Its red and gold interior has hosted some of the world's most renowned singers and conductors, and it continues to put on a high standard of performances. Inside, 200 boxes are spread over six levels. Even if you're not interested in opera, it's worth taking the guided tour. *Via San Carlo 93F.* ☎ *081/7972412. For guided tours,* ☎ *081/5534565. Tours 5€, 3€ students, Thurs–Mon 9am–5pm, Tues & Wed by appointment only.*

Orto Botanico

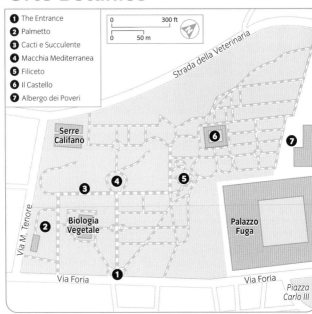

1 The Entrance
2 Palmetto
3 Cacti e Succulente
4 Macchia Mediterranea
5 Filiceto
6 Il Castello
7 Albergo dei Poveri

This walk takes you around Naples' tranquil Royal Botanical Garden, the Orto Botanico, founded by Giuseppe Bonaparte in 1807 and laid out just under the Capodimonte hill. START: **At the entrance on Via Foria 223. Walk length: 45 minutes.**

Travel Tip

Beware; there are no refreshment facilities in the Orto Botanico and nothing inviting nearby. You aren't officially allowed to picnic here, but no one minds if you bring in something to drink and a sandwich.

1 **The Entrance.** As the garden is built above street level, the main entrance takes you up a broad double staircase. To get your bearings, have a look at the map painted on ceramic tiles to your left.

Straight ahead is the wide Viale Domenico Cirillo.

2 ★ **Palmetto.** Behind the big villa on the left is the palmetto, a palm grove where species of these tropical and sub-tropical trees, in all shapes and sizes, are planted on a green lawn.

3 ★★ **Cacti e Succulente.** Near a rectangular pond full of aquatic species is the spectacular display of cacti and succulents, planted on and around a little south-facing hillock that offers maximum exposure to the sun. The examples range

About the Garden

With an area of around 30 acres (12 hectares) and situated in the chaotic Sanità neighborhood, this is one of the largest gardens of its kind in Italy. Its beautifully tended paths, smooth green lawns, and carefully laid out plant displays come as a delightful surprise in the context of smog-choked Via Foria. Today the garden is part of the university's Department of Natural Science and contains species from all over the world, laid out in reconstructions of various habitats. Everything is clearly labeled (in Italian, but the Latin names help) and cute little ceramic plaques guide you around the contrasting areas.

from mignon, furry little plants, to towering trunks with prickles that would do serious harm.

❹ ★ Macchia Mediterranea. The central area is planted with that particular combination of evergreen species typical of sunny, Mediterranean coastal areas known as *macchia mediterranea*, an aromatic combination of low-growing shrubs that includes cork oak, ilex, bay, myrtle, and rosemary.

❺ ★★★ Filiceto. Ferns thrive in a damp, shady habitat and this delightful, raised corner of the garden, protected from the sun by evergreen trees, recreates just that. A system of artificial streams and ponds guarantee a constant level of humidity. Fabulous on a hot summer day.

❻ ★ Il Castello. Turn right along the path that passes the citrus groves and you come to this mid-17th-century castle, home to a rather charming little 'Paleobotanic and Ethnobotanic' museum with displays of fossilized plantlife and artifacts fashioned from plants from all over the world.

❼ Albergo dei Poveri. The huge edifice that looms over this eastern part of the garden is the

Albergo dei Poveri, once a wretched poorhouse for the city's homeless and destitute, which was commissioned by Carlo III and built between 1751 and 1829. With a total area of some 33,455 sq. m (360,000 sq. feet) and now a UNESCO World Heritage Site, it is undergoing a major restoration.

Palm trees at the Orto Botanico.

Shopping Best Bets

Best for Neapolitan Traditional Music
★ Tattoo Records, *Piazzetta di Nilo 15 (p 72)*

Best for Prints of Old Naples
★★ Bowinkel, *Piazza dei Martiri 24 (p 72)*

Best Coffee Beans
★★ Bar Mexico, *Piazza Dante 86 (p 19)*

Best for Books in English
★★★ Feltrinelli, *Piazza dei Martiri 23 (p 72)*

Best for a Neapolitan Coffee Machine
★★ Spina, *Via Pignasecca 62 (p 74)*

Best for Cashmere
★★ Capua, *Via Bisignano 5 (p 73)*

Best for Bored Kids
★ Disney Store, *Via Toledo 129 (p 57)*

Best Custom-made Shirts
★★★ Merolla & de l'Ero, *Via Calabritto 20 (p 73)*

Best Ties
★★★ Marinella, *Riviera di Chiaia 287 (p 73)*

Best neighborhood for Designer Labels
★★★ Chiaia, *(p 160)*

Best Street Market
★★★ Mercato Pignasecca, *Piazzetta Montesanto (p 19)*

Best Handmade Leather Bags & Accessories
★★★ Fratelli Tramontano, *Via Chiaia 149e (p 75)*

Best for Wine
★★★ Enoteca Dante, *Piazza Dante 18 (p 73)*

Best ties from Marinella.

Naples **Shopping**

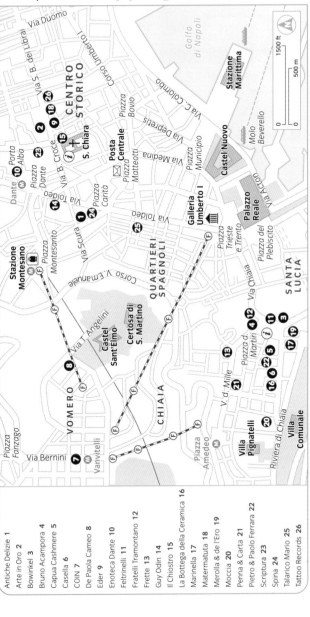

Antiche Delizie **1**
Arte in Oro **2**
Bowinkel **3**
Bruno Acampora **4**
Capua Cashmere **5**
Casella **6**
COIN **7**
De Paola Cameo **8**
Eder **9**
Enoteca Dante **10**
Feltrinelli **11**
Fratelli Tramontano **12**
Frette **13**
Guy Odin **14**
Il Chiostro **15**
La Bottega della Ceramica **16**
Marinella **17**
Matermatuta **18**
Merolla & de l'Ero **19**
Moccia **20**
Penna & Carta **21**
Pietro & Paolo Ferrara **22**
Scriptura **23**
Spina **24**
Talarico Mario **25**
Tattoo Records **26**

Naples **Shopping A to Z**

Old-fashioned Bowinkel.

Art & Antiques

★★ **Bowinkel** CHIAIA Old-fashioned Bowinkel stocks prints and watercolors of old Naples (both originals and reproductions), old photos, postcards, frames, and knick-knacks; everything is made in the city. *Piazza dei Martiri 24.* ☎ *081/7644344. AE, DC, MC, V. Bus C4, E6. Map p 71.*

★ **Casella** CHIAIA This glowing shop is an Aladdin's cave of rare and antique books. The model sailing ship in the window is for sale, too. *Via Carlo Poerio 92.* ☎ *081/7642627. AE, DC, MC, V. Bus C4, E6. Map p 71.*

Beauty Products

★★ **Bruno Acampora** CHIAIA Master perfumer to the stars, Bruno Acampora produces exquisite scents plus lotions and potions for the body and hair, all packaged in distinctive aluminum bottles. *Via Filangieri 72.* ☎ *081/401701. AE, DC, MC, V. Bus C4, E6. Map p 71.*

★ **Il Chiostro** CENTRO STORICO This little shop, located just outside Santa Chiara's cloister, stocks the beautifully packaged and reasonably priced range of bath and body goodies made by Erbolario. You'll also find herbal remedies, tisanes, and some organic produce. *Via Santa Chiara 5.* ☎ *081/5527938. MC, V. Metro Montesanto or Dante. Map p 71.*

Books & Music

★★★ **kids** **Feltrinelli** CHIAIA Feltrinelli has something for everyone and a good café, too. Travel guides, books about Naples, and English-language novels are in the basement where there's also a kids' section. You'll also find CDs and DVDs, a ticket agency, stationery, calendars, and greetings cards. *Piazza dei Martiri 23.* ☎ *081/2405411. AE, DC, MC, V. Funicular Montesanto. Map p 71.*

★ **Tattoo Records** CENTRO STORICO If you want the sunny sounds of a Neapolitan crooner, or some traditional tarantelle to prolong the holiday mood, this funky little shop will supply you with the right CDs. *Piazzetta di Nilo 15.* ☎ *081/5520973. MC, V. Metro Montesanto or Dante. Map p 71.*

Department Store

★★ **kids** **COIN** VOMERO COIN has an excellent household and kitchen department; the leather goods and shoes are worth a look as are the men's and women's fashions. There's also a decent selection of kid's clothes. *Via Scarlatti 86–100.* ☎ *081/5780111. AE, DC, MC, V. Metro Vanvitelli. Map p 71.*

Fashion & Accessories

★★★ **kids Capua Cashmere** CHIAIA Clothing for men, women, and children in the softest cashmere; sweaters, jackets, hats, gloves, and scarves in a range of beautiful colors. Strictly Made in Italy. *Via Bisignano 5.* ☎ *081/2481147. AE, DC, MC, V. Metro Amedeo. Map p 71.*

★★★ **Marinella** CHIAIA This Neapolitan institution sells custom-made ties using the finest fabrics. The tiny shop was founded in 1914 and numbers the likes of Aristotle Onassis and Giovanni Agnelli among past clients. *Riviera di Chiaia 287A.* ☎ *081/2451182. AE, DC, MC, V. Bus C4, C28, E6. Map p 71.*

★★★ **Merolla & de l'Ero** CHIAIA *The* place to go to order custom-made men's (and women's) shirts. Around 10 people take three weeks to make up any single shirt; you can choose from dozens of fine cottons, collar styles, and buttons. *Via Calabritto 20.* ☎ *081/7643012. AE, DC, MC, V. Bus C4, C28, E6. Map p 71.*

Food & Drink

★★ **Antiche Delizie** TOLEDO Just off the main Pignasecca drag, this little gastronomia sells cheeses, meats, olives, and other picnic food, and also offers great dishes to go such as lasagne. *Via Pasquale Scura 14.* ☎ *081/5513088. No credit cards. Metro Montesanto. Map p 71.*

★ **Eder** CENTRO STORICO If you can manage to squeeze past the packets of multicolored pastas and other goodies blocking the entrance way to this little shop, you will find a great source of foodie gifts. *Via Benedetto Croce 44.* ☎ *081/5517091. No credit cards. Metro Montesanto. Map p 71.*

★★★ **Enoteca Dante** TOLEDO The knowledgeable owner of this wine shop will help you choose from a great selection of well-priced Campania wines; Falanghina, Greco di Tufo, Coda di Volpi, Lachrimae Cristi, and Aglianico. *Piazza Dante 18.* ☎ *081/5499689. AE, MC, V. Metro Dante. Map p 71.*

★★★ **Guy Odin** TOLEDO Artisan chocolate maker Guy Odin has been in business since 1922, and this wonderfully old-fashioned shop is just one of several he operates in Naples. Choose from a solid chocolate Vesuvius, pralines with chili or rum and cream, and chocolate mussels filled with almond cream. *Via Toledo 214.* ☎ *081/5513491. AE, DC, MC, V. Metro Montesanto. Map p 71.*

★★ **Moccia** CHIAIA Ever-popular Moccia sells delicious rum-infused *babà*, tiny tartlets filled with wild strawberries, profiteroles, *sfogliatelle*, and ricotta-filled *cannoli*. Eat in or take away. *Via San Pasquale a Chiaia 21–22.* ☎ *081/411348. AE, MC, V. Metro Amedeo. Bus C4, C28. Map p 71.*

Homeware & Ceramics

★★★ **Frette** CHIAIA The famous Italian bedlinen company sells

Port'Alba's used book stalls.

Christmas Cribs

Neapolitan artisans have been known for their manufacture of *Presepi* or Nativity scenes for hundreds of years, but it was in the 18th century that the tradition reached its zenith. Artisans would fashion extraordinarily lifelike figurines out of wood and terracotta that were dressed by the finest tailors. They would then be placed in the context of the nativity scene complete with animals, angels, food, and drink. Today's experts, mostly based around Via San Gregorio Armeno, which turns into a big Christmas crib in early December, keep the tradition alive and have added working parts. Much of it is mass-produced these days, but if you're interested in buying quality not quantity, try **Giuseppe and Marco Ferrigno,** Via San Gregorio Armeno 10 and 55 (☎ 081/5523148) and **Cantone e Costabile,** Via Benedetto Croce 38 (☎ 081/5591186).

exquisite sheets, towels, and bedcovers in linen and cotton at its Naples branch. Prices are high; try the sales (Jan/Feb and July/Aug) for a bargain. *Via dei Mille 2.* ☎ *081/ 418728. AE, DC, MC, V. Metro Amadeo. Map p 71.*

★ La Bottega della Ceramica
CHIAIA   This little shop is crammed with colorful, traditional ceramics

Mouthwatering Antiche Delizie.

in bright, sunny colors. You'll find plates and serving dishes, vases, tiles, and lamps. *Via Carlo Poerio 41.* ☎ *081/7642626. AE, MC, V. Bus C4, E6. Map p 71.*

★★ Spina TOLEDO   An old-fashioned kitchen and hardware shop in the Pignasecca market area, Spina is famous for its coffee makers; come here for your quite portable Neapolitan version to take home. *Via Pignasecca 62.* ☎ *081/ 5524818. No credit cards. Metro Montesanto, Dante. Map p 71.*

Jewelry
★★★ Arte in Oro CENTRO
STORICO   Nothing has changed in decades at this little shop, which sells exquisite reproductions of period cameos and Roman pieces plus antique gold, silver, and coral jewelry. *Via Benedetto Croce 20.* ☎ *081/ 5516980. No credit cards. Metro Montesanto or Dante. Map p 71.*

★ De Paola Cameo VOMERO
A traditional cameo is a very nice keepsake of Naples, and this factory (near Castel Sant'Elmo) makes a vast range in various sizes and colors. *Via*

A Caccavello 67. ☎ 081/5782910. AE, D, MC, V. *Funicular to Piazza Fuga, Via Cimarosa or Kerbaker. Map p 71.*

★★ **Matermatuta** CENTRO STORICO This small shop showcases contemporary pieces made by young, local artisans from bronze, silver, and copper with semi-precious stones, natural pearls, glass, and bone. Affordable prices. *Via Benedetto Croce 38.* ☎ 081/5424315. MC, V. *Metro Montesanto or Dante. Map p 71.*

Shoes & Leather
★★★ **Fratelli Tramontano** CHIAIA This family business designs and produces exquisite handmade leather articles from belts to suitcases; past customers include Woody Allen and Tom Cruise. They also design and make articles to order. *Via Chiaia 149e.* ☎ 081/414758. AE, DC, MC, V. *Bus C4, E3, E6. Map p 71.*

★ **Pietro & Paolo Ferrara** CHIAIA The best place to buy those simple, flat and achingly chic Capri sandals is obviously Capri, but this shop selling 'Capri-style' handmade sandals, mules, and moccasins in a rainbow of colors is a good alternative. *Via Bisignano 49.*

☎ 081/7640901. Open Mar–Sept. AE, DC, MC, V. *Metro Amedeo. Map p 71.*

Stationery
★★ **Penna & Carta** CHIAIA This shop sells fine quality stationery, beautiful fountain pens and pens in hand-blown glass, art supplies, and all sorts of accessories for desk and briefcase. *Largo Vasto a Chiaia 86.* ☎ 081/418724. AE, MC, V. *Metro Amedeo. Map p 71.*

★ **Scriptura** CENTRO STORICO The family of craftspeople that own this shop make and sell leather-bound books, diaries, and albums, as well as a selection of leather bags, briefcases, and accessories. *Via San Sebastiano 22.* ☎ 081/299226. AE, MC, V. *Metro Montesanto or Dante. Map p 71.*

Umbrellas
★★ **Talarico Mario** TOLEDO This artisan shop, founded in 1860, is truly one of a kind: beautiful umbrellas are handmade on the premises in silk and wood. *Vico Due Porte a Toledo 4B.* ☎ 081/407723. AE, DC, MC, V. *Funicular Augusteo. Map p 71.*

Street Markets

Markets always offer a colorful taste of local life. La Pignasecca (see p 19, ④), the biggest and best, is the place to see the Neapolitans at their most theatrical; they flock here daily to buy anything from great hunks of swordfish and bunches of sweet Vesuvius tomatoes to fake Prada bags and cut-price perfumes. Daily **Porta Nolana** market (near Piazza Garibaldi) is another lively place, but the guys selling contraband DVDs and cigarettes threaten to outnumber the legitimate vendors. The morning market (Monday to Saturday) in **Via San Pasquale** in Chiaia is a much more civilized affair, selling fruit and vegetables plus clothes, bags, and shoes to the smart local residents. For clothing bargains, try the daily morning **Mercatino di Antignano** in Piazza degli Artisti, Vomero.

Dining Best Bets

Best for Fish
★★★ Dora $$$ *Via Ferdinando Palasciano 30 (p 79)*

Best Pizza
★★★ Da Michele $ *Via Sersale 1 (p 78);* and ★★ Marino $ *Via Santa Lucia 118 (p 80)*

Best Food With a View
★ Rosiello $$$ *Via Santo Spirito 10, Posillipo (p 81);* and ★★★ George's at Parker's $$$$ *Corso Vittorio Emanuele 135 (p 79)*

Best Ice Cream
★★★ Gelateria della Scimmia $ *Piazza Carità 4 (p 12)*

Best Sfogliatella
★★★ Scaturchio $ *Piazza San Domenico Maggiore (p 61);* and Moccia $ *Via San Pasquale a Chiaia 21–22 (p 73)*

Europeo di Mattozzi serves delicious traditional dishes.

Best Friggitoria
★★★ Fiorenzano $ *Via Ninni 1–3 (p 19)*

Best Cup of Coffee
★★★ Bar Mexico $ *Piazza Dante 86 (p 19)*

Best Budget Meal
★★★ Da Tonino $ *Via Santa Teresa a Chiaia 47 (p 78)*

Best Traditional Neapolitan Restaurant
★★★ Europeo di Mattozzi $$ *Via Campodisola Marchese 4 (p 79)*

Best for Carnivores
★★ Amici Miei $$ *Via Monte di Dio 78 (p 78)*

Best for a Romantic Dinner
★★ Rosiello $$ *Via Santo Strato 10, Posillipo (p 81)*

Best for Dinner with Bright Young Things
★★ Radici $$$ *Riviera di Chiaia 268 (p 81)*

Best Lunch Deal
★★ Il Garum $$ *Piazza Monteoliveto 2/a (p 79)*

Best Waterside Terrace
★★ Al Farretto $$ *Via Marechiaro 127 (p 78);* and ★ La Bersagliera $$$ *Borgo Marinaro 10–11 (p 79)*

Best for Impressing Your Date
★★★ George's $$$ *Corso Vittorio Emanuele 135 (p 79)*

Best Wine List
★★ La Cantina di Triunfo $$ *Riviera di Chiaia 64 (p 79)*

Best for a Business Lunch
★★ La Cantinella $$$ *Via Nazario Sauro 23 (p 80)*

Naples **Dining**

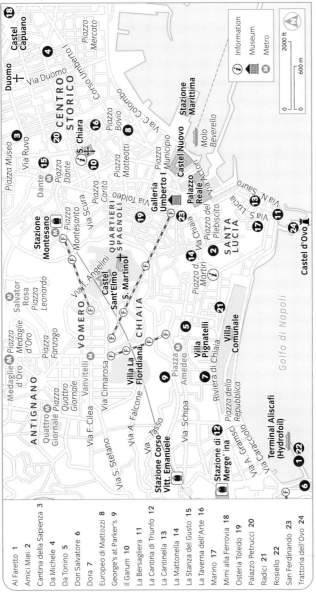

Al Faretto 1
Amici Miei 2
Cantina della Sapienza 3
Da Michele 4
Da Tonino 5
Don Salvatore 6
Dora 7
Europeo di Mattozzi 8
George's at Parker's 9
Il Garum 10
La Bersagliera 11
La Cantina di Triunfo 12
La Cantinella 13
La Mattonella 14
La Stanza del Gusto 15
La Taverna dell'Arte 16
Marino 17
Mimi alla Ferrovia 18
Osteria Toledo 19
Palazzo Petrucci 20
Radici 21
Rosiello 22
San Ferdinando 23
Trattoria dell'Ovo 24

Naples Dining A to Z

★★ **Al Faretto** MARECHIARO *FISH & PIZZA* Take a break from the city and head to this stylish waterside restaurant in the tiny fishing village of Marechiaro, a perfect spot for lunch on a sunny day. *Via Marechiaro 127.* ☎ *081/5750407. Entrees 10–18€, pizza 4.50–7€. Lunch & dinner Tues–Sun. Bus C23 or taxi. Map p 77.*

★★ **Amici Miei** ROYAL NAPLES *ITALIAN* Carnivores will enjoy this excellent restaurant where there's not a fish in sight. Tuck into the likes of curry-spiked risotto with goose breast and chargrilled steak complemented by fine wines. *Via Monte di Dio 78.* ☎ *081/7646063. Entrees 7.50–16€. AE, DC, MC, V. Lunch Tues–Sun, dinner Tues–Sat; closed July & Aug. Bus E3, E6. Map p 77.*

★ **Cantina della Sapienza** CENTRO STORICO *TRADITIONAL* This popular, rustic little eatery serves good, home-cooked food such as meat balls in tomato sauce and eggplant parmesan, plus a great choice of vegetables. *Via della Sapienza 40.* ☎ *081/459078. Entrees 3–7€. No credit cards. Lunch Mon–Sat; closed 3 weeks in Aug. Metro Cavour. Map p 77.*

★★★ **kids** **Da Michele** CORSO UMBERTO/STATION *PIZZA* Take a number and join the queue for what many believe to be the best pizza in town. Choice is limited to margherita or marinara, and the place is extremely Spartan, but this is a truly Neapolitan experience that shouldn't be missed. *Via Sersale 1.* ☎ *081/5539204. Pizzas 4–5€. No credit cards. Mon–Sat 10am–midnight. Metro Garibaldi. Map p 77.*

★★ **Da Tonino** CHIAIA *TRADITIONAL* A combination of home-style cooking, such as lentil soup and squid in tomato sauce, unbeatable prices, and simpatico owner Tonino's endless chatter means that this simple little trattoria is always packed. *Via Santa Teresa a Chiaia 47.* ☎ *081/421533. Entrees 3–6€. No credit cards. Lunch Mon–Sat,*

Da Tonino: a taste of Old Naples.

dinner Fri & Sat; closed Aug. Bus C4, C26, C28. Map p 77.

★★ **Don Salvatore** MERGELLINA *FISH & PIZZA* Although pizza and meat dishes feature on the menu of this elegant restaurant, I recommend fish and seafood specialties such as pasta with lobster and sea bass with caper sauce. *Via Mergellina 5.* ☎ *081/681817. Entrees 14.50–20€. AE, DC, MC, V. Lunch & dinner Thurs–Tues. Metro Mergellina. Bus 140, R3. Map p 77.*

★★★ **Dora** CHIAIA *FISH* Tiny Dora's has a cult following among both locals and visitors, who cram in for unpretentious (but expensive) dishes based on the freshest fish. Ihad a superb plate of spaghetti with clams here. *Via Ferdinando Palasciano 30.* ☎ *081/680519. Entrees 15–40€. MC, V. Lunch & dinner Mon–Sat. Bus 140, 152, C28. Map p 77.*

★★★ **Europeo di Mattozzi** PORT *TRADITIONAL & PIZZA* Alfonso Mattozzi's comfortingly old-fashioned trattoria is one of the city's best, and a personal favorite. Top-notch ingredients go into Neapolitan staples such as lentil and *friarielli* (a kind of bitter greens) soup and *paccheri* (large pasta tubes) with mixed seafood. *Via Campodisola Marchese 4.* ☎ *081/5521323. Entrees 10–18€. AE, MC, V. Lunch Mon, Tues, lunch & dinner Wed–Sat. Bus 201, E1, E2, R4. Map p 77.*

★★★ **George's at Parker's** VOMERO *GOURMET* Located on the top floor of Grand Hotel Parker's, George's is not only one of the most panoramic restaurants in Naples, but also among the best. Chef 'Baciòt' bases his creative, regionally inspired menus on top-class seasonal ingredients. A treat. *Corso Vittorio Emanuele 135.* ☎ *081/7612474. Entrees 24–30€. AE, DC, MC, V. Lunch & dinner daily.*

Try George's for a special treat.

Funicular Chiaia to Corso Vittorio Emanuele. Map p 77.

★★ **Il Garum** CENTRO STORICO *CREATIVE TRADITIONAL* A good place for a cheap, central lunch (there's a 10€ set menu), Il Garum offers a pretty terrace and a light, creative take on the local cuisine. Try the rabbit with apples or 'Neapolitan sushi.' *Piazza Monteoliveto 2/a.* ☎ *081/5423228. Entrees 12–18€. AE, MC, V. Lunch & dinner daily. Metro Dante. Map p 77.*

★ **La Bersagliera** BORGO MARINARO *FISH* Lunch on the sunny terrace of this elegant place is a delight. The mussel and clam soup is a classic; follow this with a delicious fritto misto (deep fried mixed fish and seafood). *Borgo Marinaro 10–11.* ☎ *081/7646016. Entrees 8–16€. AE, DC, MC, V. Lunch & dinner Wed–Mon. Bus 152, C4. Map p 77.*

★★ **La Cantina di Triunfo** CHIAIA *WINE BAR* Best described as a wine bar with food, this tiny place offers a limited choice of excellent dishes such as bean and chestnut soup and baked fish with artichokes to complement superb wines. *Riviera di Chiaia 64.* ☎ *081/668101. Entrees 18€. AE, MC, V. Dinner Mon–Sat. Bus 140, 152, C12, C18. Map p 77.*

★★ **La Cantinella** ROYAL NAPLES *GOURMET* The combination of an elegant, rather retro atmosphere; views straight onto Vesuvius; and excellent, imaginative food make this place a good choice for a special meal out. *Via Nazario Sauro 23.* ☎ *081/7648684. Entrees 13–30€. AE, DC, MC, V. Lunch & dinner Mon–Sat; closed 2 weeks in Aug. Bus 140, 152, C4. Map p 77.*

★ **La Mattonella** ROYAL NAPLES *TRADITIONAL* A tiny, family-run trattoria that takes its name from the colorful ceramic tiles that adorn the walls, La Matonella serves good, traditional food at modest prices. *Via Nicotera 13.* ☎ *081/416541. Entrees 6–9€. No credit cards. Lunch daily, dinner Mon–Sat. Bus E3, E6. Map p 77.*

★★ **La Stanza del Gusto** CENTRO STORICO *CONTEMPORARY & WINE BAR* This arty eatery is two rolled into one: a sophisticated upstairs restaurant featuring a series of menus based on the chef's interpretations of local cuisine, and a colorful Cheese Bar where you can choose from dozens of cheeses plus hot dishes and excellent wines. *Via Santa Maria di Costantinopoli 100.* ☎ *081/401578. Tasting menus 35–65€; Cheese Bar entrées 11–16€. AE, MC, V. Lunch Tues–Sun, dinner Tues–Sat. Metro Dante. Map p 77.*

★★ **La Taverna dell'Arte** CENTRO STORICO *CREATIVE TRADITIONAL* This hard-to-find eatery has the feel of a cozy private club. The menu changes almost daily and there's always something

interesting on offer, such as stuffed calamari or sweet and sour roast pork. *Rampa San Giovanni Maggiore 1A.* ☎ *081/5527558. Entrées 7.50–15€. MC, V. Dinner Mon–Sat. Metro Dante. Map p 77.*

★★ **kids** **Marino** SANTA LUCIA *FISH & PIZZA* A typical example of a modest, neighborhood pizzeria, old-fashioned Marino is convenient if you're staying on the Santa Lucia waterfront. It serves great pizza plus seafood pasta and main courses. *Via Santa Lucia 118.* ☎ *081/7640280. Pizza 4–8€, entrees 7–9€. AE, DC, MC, V. Lunch & dinner Tues–Sun; closed Aug. Bus 140, 152, C4. Map p 77.*

★★ **Mimi alla Ferrovia** CORSO UMBERTO/STATION *FISH* Beloved by visiting celebrities, this Neapolitan classic serves great food at fair prices. Try the delicious antipasti and *paccheri* with monkfish and cherry tomatoes. *Via Alfonso D'Aragona 19–21.* ☎ *081/289004. Entrees 13–18€. AE, MC, V. Dinner Mon–Sat. Metro Garibaldi. Map p 77.*

kids **Osteria Toledo** TOLEDO *TRADITIONAL* This Quartieri Spagnoli *osteria* has been dishing up wholesome home cooking since 1951. Staples such as pasta with meat sauce and *fritto misto* (deep fried mixed seafood) are served off red-and-white checked cloths. *Vico Giardinetto a Toledo 78.* ☎ *081/421257. Entrees 4.50–12€. MC, V. Lunch daily, dinner Wed–Mon. Bus E3, E6. Map p 77.*

★★ **Palazzo Petrucci** CENTRO STORICO *CONTEMPORARY* This stylish restaurant, housed in a former stables, serves Neapolitan cuisine with a creative twist; try the lasagne with buffalo mozzarella, shrimp, zucchini flowers, and pesto. Good wine list, too. *Piazza San Domenico Maggiore 4.* ☎ *081/5524068. Entrees 14–18€. AE, DC, MC, V. Lunch*

Tues–Sun, dinner Tues–Sat. Metro
Dante. Map p 77.

★★ **Radici** CHIAIA *CONTEMPO-
RARY* With its contemporary decor
and light-handed take on traditional
Neapolitan cuisine, Radici is not just
a hangout for the city's beautiful
people: the food is seriously good.
Menus are based on seasonal avail-
ability and there's a wine list that
features labels from all over Italy.
Riviera di Chiaia 268. ☎ *081/
2481100. Entrees 16–21€. AE, DC,
MC, V. Lunch Fri & Sat, dinner Mon–
Sat. Metro Amedeo. Map p 77.*

★★ **Rosiello** POSILLIPO *FISH &
PIZZA* Rosiello's hillside position
offers a unique, panoramic backdrop
for meals on its flower-filled terraces.
Classic dishes (mostly fish-based) are
carefully prepared and presented on
colorful ceramic plates. *Via Santo
Strato 10, Posillipo.* ☎ *081/7691288.
Entrees 15–30€, pizza 6–12€. AE, DC,
MC, V. Lunch & dinner Thurs–Tues.
Bus 140,C31. Map p 77.*

★★ **San Ferdinando** TOLEDO
TRADITIONAL An excellent family-
run trattoria where you can sample
punchy, flavorful pasta dishes such
as *paccheri* with baby squid, capers,
and black olives; wash it all down
with the house *falanghina* wine,
served chilled in bright ceramic
jugs. *Via Nardones 117.* ☎ *081/
421964. Entrees 9.50–15€. AE, DC,
MC, V. Lunch Mon–Sat, dinner Wed–
Fri. Bus E3, E6. Map p 77.*

Trattoria dell'Ovo BORGO
MARINARI *TRADITIONAL* Among
all the trendy eateries of the charming Borgo Marinari, this simple little
trattoria stands out for its modest
prices and wholesome, unfussy
food. In summer, tables are laid on
the terrace overlooking the marina.
Via Luculliana 28. ☎ *081/7646352.
Entrees 5.50–9€. No credit cards.
Lunch & dinner Fri–Wed. Bus 152,
C4, B. Map p 77.*

Busy Mimi alla Ferrovia.

Naples Nightlife, Arts & Entertainment

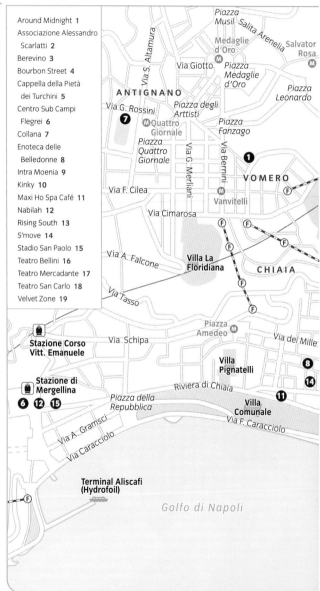

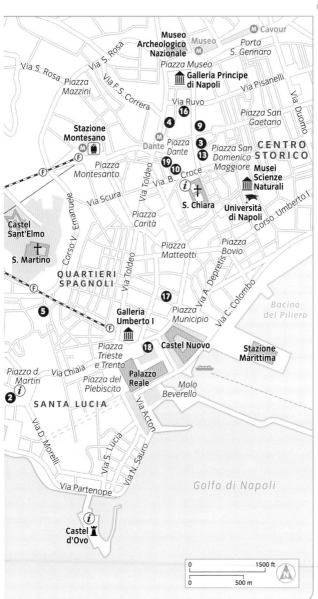

Nightlife/A&E Best Bets

Best for Grand Opera
★★★ Teatro San Carlo, *Via San Carlo 98F (p 86)*

Best for Neapolitan Baroque Opera
★★ Cappella delle Pietà dei Turchini, *Via Santa Caterina da Siena 38 (p 85)*

Best Summer Nightclub
★★★ Nabilah, *Via Spiaggia Romana 15, Fusaro (p 87)*

Best for a Late-night Glass of Wine
★★★ Enoteca Belledonne, *Vico Belledonne a Chiaia 18 (p 85)*

Best for Italian Theater
★ Teatro Mercadante, *Piazza Municipio 1 (p 85)*

Best Open-air Public Pool
Collana, *Via Rossini (p 87)*

Best for Live Jazz
Bourbon Street, *Via Bellini 52 (p 86)*

Best for a Tango
★ Maxi Ho Spa Cafè, *Via Carlo Poerio 47 (p 85)*

Best Student Hangouts
★★★ Piazza Bellini *(p 86)*; and ★★ Piazza San Domenico *(p 61)*

Best Upmarket Hangout
★★★ Chiaia *(p 160)*

Best Cool Bar/Club
★★★ S'move, *Vico dei Sospiri 10 (p 85)*

Best Central Dance Venue
★★★ Velvet Zone, *Via Cisterna dell'Olio 11 (p 87)*

Best Way to See the Local Dive Sites
Centro Sub Campi Flegrei, *Via Napoli 1, Pozzuoli (p 87)*

Best Place to See the Home Team Win
★★★ Stadio San Paolo, *Piazzale Teccio, Fuorigrotta (p 87)*

Most Gay-friendly Bars
★★ Any in Piazza Bellini, including Intra Moenia *Piazza Bellini 70 (p 85)*

Best Grand Café
★★ Grand Caffé Gambrinus, *Via Chiaia 1 (p 11)*

Nightlife spills out onto the street in Chiaia.

Naples Nightlife/A&E A to Z

Ticket Tip

The following sites handle online ticket sales for music and theater events all over Italy: www.charta.it, www.helloticket.it, and www.vivaticket.it. Hello Italy also handles phone sales (some English spoken). ☎ 800/907080.

Bars & Lounges

★ **Berevino** CENTRO STORICO   A stylish wine bar and general student hangout that offers a good selection of wines plus snacks (or dinner) well into the night. *Via San Sebastiano 62.* ☎ *081/290313. Metro Dante. Map p 82.*

★★ **Enoteca delle Belledonne** CHIAIA   A friendly, upmarket little wine bar that fills up early evening and stays that way until the early hours. Standing room only in the front, sit-down space in the back and overflow on the pretty street. *Vico Belledonne a Chiaia 18.* ☎ *081/403162. Metro Amadeo, Bus R3. Map p 82.*

★★ **Intra Moenia** CENTRO STORICO   One of several buzzy bars in pretty Piazza Bellini, Intra Moenia is particularly popular on balmy summer nights when the outside tables are packed. *Piazza Bellini 70.* ☎ *081/290988. Metro Dante. Map p 82.*

★ **Maxi Ho Spa Café** CHIAIA   This slick, multipurpose bar, café, and homeware shop attracts a sleek, chic crowd in the evenings. The regular program of events includes a tango night on the last Thursday of the month. *Via Carlo Poerio 47.* ☎ *081/7644619. Bus C4, E6. Map p 82.*

★★★ **S'move** CHIAIA   S'move's upscale deep red and beige decor suits its chic Chiaia location. It's a relaxed and friendly place with cool background sounds, halfway between a bar and a club. *Vico dei Sospiri 10A.* ☎ *081/7645813. www.smove-lab.net. Metro Piazza Amadeo. Map p 82.*

Classical Music, Dance & Theater

★★ **Associazione Alessandro Scarlatti**   Look out for this excellent season of classical concerts (mostly chamber music) featuring local artists and internationally known names. Venues vary, but include Villa Pignatelli and Castel Sant'Elmo. ☎ *081/406011. www.associazionescarlatti.it. Tickets 18–28€. Map p 82.*

★★ **Cappella della Pietà dei Turchini** TOLEDO   This excellent baroque music group, specializing in 17th- and 18th-century Neapolitan opera, perform regularly in the city, often in the deconsecrated church of Santa Caterina da Siena. *Via Santa Caterina da Siena 38.* ☎ *081/402395. www.turchini.it. Tickets 10€. Map p 82.*

★ **Teatro Bellini** TOLEDO   This ornate theater in the grand style puts on a regular program of musicals, dance, concerts of Neapolitan music, and some plays from October to May. *Via Conte di Ruvo 14–19.* ☎ *081/5499688. www.teatrobellini.it. Tickets 12–28€. Metro Cavour. Map p 82.*

★ **Teatro Mercadante** ROYAL NAPLES   Naples' beautiful 1779 state theater puts on plays featuring the top Italian actors and directors, but obviously has limited interest

Hanging Out With the Locals

Naples has a lively, constantly evolving nightlife scene with venues opening and closing again quicker than you can say 'pizza Margherita.' The places listed here are pretty well established, but there's plenty of scope for improvisation. The *centro storico* bars fill up quickly on Friday and Saturday nights with a mixed bag of students, and arty and alternative types. Join the crowds in the areas around Piazza San Domenico, Piazza Bellini, and Via Cisterna dell'Olio and see where they take you. Classy Chiaia caters to a more upscale crowd who gather in the numerous small, trendy bars in and around Via Fiorelli, Vico Belledonne a Chiaia, Vico dei Sospiri, and Via Bisignano.

for non-Italian speakers. *Piazza Municipio 1.* ☎ *081/5513396. www. teatrostabilenapoli.it. Tickets 8.50– 27€. Bus R1, R2, 157. Map p 82.*

★★★ Teatro San Carlo ROYAL NAPLES   One of Italy's premier opera houses, the grand, newly renovated Teatro San Carlo's opera season runs from January to

Glorious Teatro San Carlo.

December (except July and Aug). Ballet and orchestral concerts are also included in the program. *Via San Carlo 98F.* ☎ *081/7972330/ box office 081/7972331. www.teatrosan carlo.it. Tickets 30–100€. Box office Tues–Sun 10am–7pm. Bus 157, R2, E6. Map p 82.*

Jazz
Around Midnight VOMERO
A small, friendly Vomero jazz club that presents evenings of live music, mainly jazz. There's hot and cold food, cocktails, beers, and wine. *Via Bonito 32A.* ☎ *081/7423278. www. aroundmidnight.it. Cover Wed & Thurs 2.50€, Fri–Sun 5€. Closed July & Aug. Metro Vanvitelli. Map p 82.*

★ Bourbon Street CENTRO STORICO   This popular *centro storico* jazz club puts on nightly live music, mostly featuring local line-ups. *Via Bellini 52.* ☎ *338/8253756. Tues–Sun 9pm–3am. Metro Dante. Map p 82.*

Nightclubs
★ Kinky TOLEDO   Kinky is the best venue in Naples to hear reggae sounds. The DJ spins his tunes out front while the backroom dance

space fills to crush level. *Via Cisterna dell'Olio 21.* ☎ *081/5521571, 335/5477299. www.kinkyjam.com. No cover. Closed mid-June–mid-Sep. Metro Dante. Map p 82.*

★★★ **Nabilah** FUSARO This gorgeous seaside venue is one of Naples' best summer nightspots. Kick off your shoes; dancing here is done on the sand and the cool, contemporary ambiance is more Ibiza than Campania. Trains stop early, so either go back to town after a cocktail, or stay up all night. *Via Spiaggia Romana 15, Fusaro.* ☎ *081/8689433. Cover 10–20€; includes 1 drink. Open May–Sep Fri, Sat 9pm–4am, Sun 6pm–4am. Cumana Rail to Torre Gaveta. Map p 82.*

★★ **Rising South** CENTRO STORICO This club occupies an atmospheric, long, tunnel-like space with a stone barrel-vault ceiling. Armchairs and sofas encourage lounging (as do the sounds); there's contemporary art on the walls and good drinks. A very cool place. *Via San Sebastiano 19.* ☎ *335/8790428. www.risingrepublic.com. Annula membership 10€. Closed mid-May–mid-Sep. Metro Dante. Map p 82.*

★★★ **Velvet Zone** CENTRO STORICO Don't even think of arriving at central Naples' best dance venue before 1am. The basement rooms are smoky and atmospheric and the dance floor is always packed for DJ sounds that range from techno to '80s revivals. *Via Cisterna dell'Olio 11.* ☎ *328/9577115 or 339/6700234. Cover 10€. Closed mid-May–mid-Sep. Metro Dante. Map p 82.*

Sports
★★ **Centro Sub Campi Flegrei** BAIA This center offers excursions to the submerged city of ancient Baiae (see p 25, ⑥), a wonderful

Velvet Zone is strictly for night owls.

great dive site. *Via Napoli 1, Pozzuoli.* ☎ *081/8531563. www.centro subcampiflegrei.it. Metro Pozzuoli or Cumana rail to Gerolamini. Map p 82.*

kids Collana VOMERO This municipally owned outdoor pool opens from June to September and is one of the few pools in town that you can use without taking out membership. *Via Rossini, Vomero.* ☎ *081/5601988. Metro Quattro Giornate. Map p 82.*

★★★ **kids Stadio San Paolo** FUORIGROTTA The Neapolitans are soccer (*calcio*) crazy and flock to the city's 80,000-seater stadium in Fuorigrotta to watch the home team Napoli play on alternate Sundays between September and May. *Piazzale Teccio, Fuorigrotta. Tickets from Azzurro Service, Via F Galeota 17, Fuorigrotta.* ☎ *081/5934001. Cuma rail to Mostra. Map p 82.*

Naples Lodging

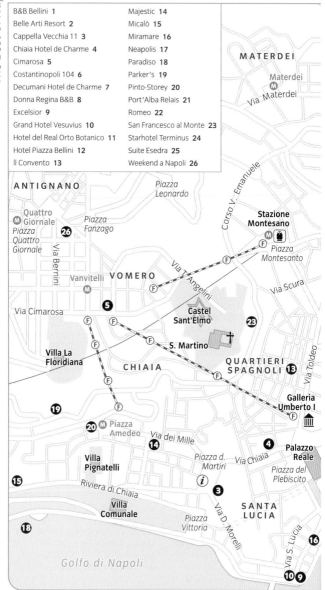

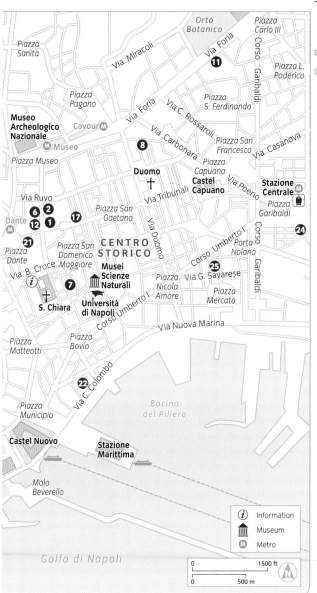

Lodging Best Bets

Grand Hotel Vesuvius.

Best Boutique Hotels
★★★ Costantinopoli 104 \$\$ *Via Costantinopoli 104 (p 91)*; and ★★★ Micalò \$\$ *Riviera di Chiaia 88 (p 93)*

Best Budget Hotel
★★ Hotel Piazza Bellini \$ *Via Costantinopoli 101 (p 92)*

Best for Star-spotting
★★★ Grand Hotel Vesuvius \$\$\$\$ *Via Partenope 45 (p 92)*

Best Rooftop Pool
★★★ San Francesco al Monte \$\$\$ *Corso Vittorio Emanuele 328 (p 94)*

Best Spaccanapoli Location
★ Decumani Hotel de Charme \$\$ *Via San Giovanni Maggiore Pignatelli 15 (p 91)*

Best for Chic Shoppers
★★ Majestic \$\$\$ *Largo Vasto a Chiaia 68 (p 92)*

Best In-house Spa
★★★ Romeo \$\$\$\$ *Via Cristoforo Colombo 45 (p 93)*

Best Home-cooked Breakfast
★★★ Micalò \$\$ *Riviera di Chiaia 88 (p 93)*; and ★★ Donna Regina B&B \$ *Via Luigi Settembrini 80 (p 92)*

Best Hotel Garden
★★★ Costantinopoli 104 \$\$ *Via Costantinopoli 104 (p 91)*

Best Homely B&Bs
★★ Donna Regina B&B \$ *Via Luigi Settembrini 80 (p 92)*; and ★★ Weekend a Napoli \$\$ *Via E Alvino 157 (p 94)*

Best for Out and Out Luxury
★★★ Romeo \$\$\$\$ *Via Cristoforo Colombo 45 (p 93)*; and ★★★ Grand Hotel Vesuvius \$\$\$\$ *Via Partenope 45 (p 92)*

Best for Catching an Early Train
★ Starhotel Terminus \$\$\$ *Piazza Garibaldi 91 (p 94)*

Best for Gourmets
★★★ Parker's \$\$\$\$ *Corso Vittorio Emanuele 135 (p 93)*

Best Volcanic Views
★★ Miramare \$\$\$ *Via Nazario Sauro 24m (p 93)*

Best for Business
★ Star Hotel Terminus \$\$\$ *Piazza Garibaldi 91 (p 94)*

Best for Families
★★ Weekend a Napoli \$\$ *Via E Alvino 157 (p 94)*

Naples Lodging A to Z

★★ B&B Bellini CENTRO STORICO Occupying a bright, homey apartment that was once part of a convent, the Bellini has three comfortable rooms with mosaic bathrooms and a pretty, flower-filled terrace for breakfast. *Piazza Bellini 68.* ☎ *081/0607338. www.bbbellini.it. 3 units. Doubles 80–100€ w/breakfast. MC, V. Metro Dante. Map p 89.*

★★ Belle Arti Resort CENTRO STORICO A small, stylish hotel offering a tasteful mix of old and new; ceiling frescoes and original fittings mix with flat screen TVs, contemporary art, and modern bathrooms. *Via Santa Maria di Costantinopoli 27.* ☎ *081/5571062. www.belleartiresort.com. 7 units. Doubles 80–160€ w/breakfast. AE, MC, V. Metro Dante. Map p 89.*

★★ Cappella Vecchia 11 CHIAIA This friendly B&B is located in an impressive palazzo. The bright, modern rooms have wood floors and mosaic bathrooms. *Vico Santa Maria a Cappella Vecchia 11.* ☎ *081/2405117. www.bednaples.com. 6 units. Doubles 75–120€ w/breakfast. AE, MC, V. Bus 152, C4, E6. Map p 89.*

★★ Chiaia Hotel de Charme CHIAIA Partly housed in a former brothel and located off a quiet courtyard, this hotel offers elegant, comfortable rooms and attentive, friendly service. *Via Chiaia 216.* ☎ *081/415555. www.hotelchiaia.it. 33 units. Doubles 99–195€ w/breakfast. AE, D, MC, V. Bus E3, E6. Map p 89.*

★★ Cimarosa VOMERO This hotel in peaceful, bourgeois Vomero offers stylish, contemporary decor and good prices. Not all rooms have en suite bathrooms. *Via Cimarosa*

B&B Bellini.

29. ☎ *081/5567044. 18 units. Doubles 70–130€ w/breakfast. MC, V. Metro Vanvitelli or funicular to Via Morghen. Map p 89.*

★★★ Costantinopoli 104 CENTRO STORICO This delightful hotel is accessed through a garden with a small pool. Inside, it is cool and sleek with beautifully appointed rooms featuring tiled floors, antiques, and smart marble bathrooms. *Via Costantinopoli 104.* ☎ *081/5571035. www.costantinopoli104.it. 19 units. Doubles 170–250€ w/breakfast. AE, D, MC, V. Metro Dante. Map p 89.*

★ Decumani Hotel de Charme CENTRO STORICO This refined little hotel occupies an ex-bishop's palace; the elegant rooms feature antiques and original stuccowork. *Via San Giovanni Maggiore Pignatelli 15.* ☎ *081/5518188. www.decumani.com. 24 units. Doubles 99–144€ w/breakfast. AE, D, MC, V. Metro Montesanto, Bus R2. Map p 89.*

Belle-Epoque elegance, Costantinopoli 104.

★★★ Donna Regina B&B CEN-
TRO STORICO A homely B&B
housed in an ex-convent, Donna
Regina is filled with family antiques
and pictures. A delicious breakfast
(plus other meals on request) is
served in the old tiled kitchen. *Via
Luigi Settembrini 80.* ☎ *081/446799.
www.discovernaples.net. 5 units.
Doubles 93€ w/breakfast. AE, MC, V.
Metro Cavour. Map p 89.*

★★★ Excelsior WATERFRONT
With its sister hotel Vesuvius, the
lovely old Excelsior shares prime
waterside frontage opposite the
Castel dell'Ovo, and is favored by
VIPs. Rooms have antiques, fine fabrics, and marble bathrooms. The
rooftop terrace is a fabulous spot
for a romantic dinner, drinks, or sunbathing. *Via Partenope 48.* ☎ *081/
7640111. www.excelsior.it. 123
units. Doubles 260–390€. AE, DC,
MC, V. Bus 140, 152. Map p 89.*

★★★ Grand Hotel Vesuvius
WATERFRONT Hiding behind a
bland modern façade, one of
Naples' oldest hotels has hosted
kings and movie stars. It boasts luxurious classic rooms with sea views,
a spa, a rooftop restaurant, and a
private yacht available for hire. All
that and top-class service, too. *Via
Partenope 45.* ☎ *081/7640044.*

*www.vesuvio.it. 120 units. Doubles
290–450€. AE, DC, MC, V. Bus 140,
152. Map p 89.*

★ Hotel del Real Orto Botanico
SANITÀ Overlooking the botanical
gardens and only ½ km (⅓ mile)
from the famous archeological
museum, this friendly hotel has
comfortable rooms, a roof garden,
and a courtyard restaurant serving
local fare. *Via Foria 192.* ☎ *081/
4421528. www.hotelrealorto
botanico.it. 36 units. Doubles
80–160€ w/breakfast. MC, V.
Metro Cavour. Map p 89.*

★ kids Hotel Piazza Bellini
CENTRO STORICO Occupying an
18th-century palazzo, this hotel
offers minimalist, contemporary
bedrooms with designer furniture,
wood floors and slick bathrooms.
Some rooms have balconies overlooking the piazza. *Via Costantinopoli 101.* ☎ *081/451732. www.
hotelpiazzabellini.com. 50 units.
Doubles 75–130€ w/breakfast. AE,
DC, MC, V, Metro Dante. Map p 89.*

★ Il Convento TOLEDO Housed
in an ex-convent, this friendly little
hotel has preserved monastic features such as plain walls, wood ceilings, stone floors and arches, but
there are modern comforts too. *Via
Speranzella 137A.* ☎ *081/403977.
www.hotelilconvento.com. 10 units.
Doubles 65–150€ w/breakfast. AE,
D,MC,V. Bus R2. Map p 89.*

★ Majestic CHIAIA This modern
hotel enjoys an excellent location
in the heart of the Chiaia shopping
district. The pleasant, traditional
rooms are spread over 10 floors and
there's a good restaurant serving
creative food. *Largo Vasto a Chiaia
68.* ☎ *081/416500. www.majestic.it.
102 units. Doubles 160–280€. AE, D,
MC, V. Metro Amedeo, Bus C4, C26,
C28. Map p 89.*

★★★ **Micalò** CHIAIA   This stylish little boutique hotel is an oasis of calm. Simple yet chic rooms feature iroko wood and pale stone. A delicious breakfast and light meals are on offer. *Riviera di Chiaia 88.* ☎ *081/7617131. www.micalo.it. 9 units. Doubles 165–240€ w/breakfast. AE, DC, MC, V. Bus 140, 152, C12, C18. Map p 89.*

★★ **Miramare** ROYAL NAPLES   Small, family-run Miramare occupies a Liberty villa on the waterfront with full-on views of Mt. Vesuvius, best enjoyed from the rooftop terrace. With its very personalized decor, it has the atmosphere of a private home. *Via Nazario Sauro 24.* ☎ *081/7647589. www.hotelmiramare.com. 30 units. Doubles 149–299€ w/breakfast. AE, DC, MC, V. Bus 152. Map p 89.*

★ **Neapolis** CENTRO STORICO   The modern rooms of this hotel are each supplied with a computer and free Internet access. Prices are good, the staff is very friendly, and discounts are offered at the adjoining traditional restaurant. *Via Francesco del Giudice 13.* ☎ *081/4420815. www.hotelneapolis.com. 24 units. 76–122€ w/breakfast. AE, DC, MC, V. Metro Cavour or Dante. Map p 89.*

★★ kids **Paradiso** POSILLIPO   If you want to escape to the hills after a chaotic day in central Naples, the Paradiso a good choice. Its location guarantees panoramic views over Mt. Vesuvius and the bay, and many of its sunny rooms have terraces. *Via Catullo 11.* ☎ *081/2475111. www.hotelparadisonapoli.it. 72 units. Doubles 80–230€ w/breakfast. AE, DC, MC, V. Funicular Mergellina to San Gioachino. Map p 89.*

★★★ **Parker's** VOMERO   Parker's has old-world charm by the bucketload and a fine rooftop restaurant (see p 79). The neoclassical style

Cool, contemporary style at Micalò.

features antiques, chandeliers, and sumptuous fabrics: make sure you ask for a room with a view. *Corso Vittorio Emanuele 135.* ☎ *081/7612474. www.grandhotelparkers.com. 82 units. Doubles 200–360€ w/breakfast. AE, DC, MC, V. Funicular Chiaia to Corso Vittorio Emanuele. Map p 89.*

★ **Pinto-Storey** CHIAIA   Housed on the upper floors of a lovely old Liberty palazzo, the Pinto-Storey has managed to maintain its old-fashioned atmosphere in spite of recent renovation. *Via G Martucci 72.* ☎ *081/681260. www.pintostorey.it. 16 units. Double 88–173€ w/breakfast. AE, MC, V. Metro Amedeo. Map p 89.*

★★ **Port'Alba Relais** CENTRO STORICO   All six rooms at this stylish little guesthouse overlook bustling Piazza Dante. Rooms are done out in soft gray and cream with original wood ceilings and smart bathrooms. *Via Port'Alba 33.* ☎ *081/5645171. www.portalberelais.com. 6 units. Doubles 90–150€ w/breakfast. AE, MC, V. Metro Dante. Map p 89.*

★★★ **Romeo** PORT   The new-ish Romeo features luxurious high tech style and a plethora of facilities and services. Conveniently located near

San Francesco al Monte.

the tourist port and housed in the ex-headquarters of a shipping company, it is filled with one-off design classics and superb antiques. There's a gourmet restuarant and a pool on the roof, a sushi bar and a fabulous spa; guests are even offered a sheet and pillow menu. *Via Cristoforo Colombo 45. Tel 081 0175. www.romeohotel.it. 83 units. Doubles 330€. Bus 1, R2. Map p 89.*

★★ San Francesco al Monte

VOMERO   This hillside hotel combines the atmosphere of an ancient monastery with 21st-century comforts. Rooms all have sea views; two have terraces. There is a spectacular roof garden with a pool and an elegant restaurant serving a creative take on local dishes. *Corso Vittorio Emanuele 328. ☎ 081/4239111. www.hotelsanfrancesco.it. 45 units. Doubles 140–295€ w/breakfast. AE, DC, MC, V. Funicular Central to Corso Vittorio Emanuele. Map p 89.*

★ Starhotel Terminus CORSO

UMBERTO/STATION   If you want to stay near the train station, this big 4-star hotel with its sharp, contemporary decor, is an excellent choice;

you can step right off the train into your room. *Piazza Garibaldi 91. ☎ 081/7793111. www.starhotels.it. 173 units. Doubles 130–260€ w/ breakfast. AE, DC, MC, V. Metro Piazza Garibaldi. Map p 89.*

★ Suite Esedra CORSO UMBERTO/

STATION   Set back a little from noisy Corso Umberto II, the Esedra features flower-decked balconies and a cozy atmosphere. Suite Venus has a private terrace and Jacuzzi tub. *Via Cantani 12. ☎ 081/5537087. www.sea-hotels.com. 17 rooms. Doubles 65–100€ w/breakfast. AE, DC, MC, V. Metro Piazza Garibaldi. Map p 89.*

★★ kids Weekend a Napoli

VOMERO   Paolo and Patrizia offer the warmest of welcomes and homemade cakes for breakfast at this charming B&B, which occupies an elegant Liberty villa in quiet, leafy Vomero. Self-catering apartments are in the annex. *Via E Alvino 157. ☎ 081/5781010. www.weekend anapoli.com. 6 units. Doubles 133–193€ w/breakfast. AE, MC, V. Map p 89.* ●

The Best in **Three Days**

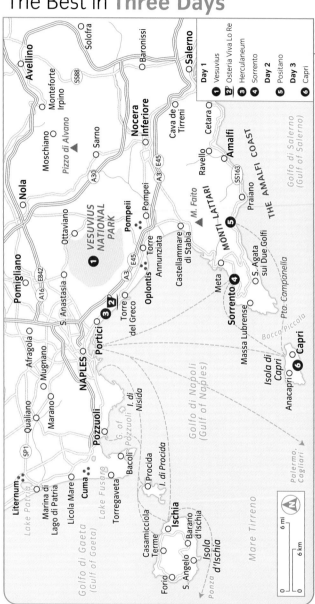

Day 1
1 Vesuvius
2 Osteria Viva Lo Re
3 Herculaneum
4 Sorrento

Day 2
5 Positano

Day 3
6 Capri

Previous page: Positano

I f you have only three days in which to see the area, all is not lost. Distances are contained and there's a bit of everything within a short radius: ancient culture, staggering scenery, island life, and glamorous towns. START: **Naples.**

Head out of Naples on the A3 autostrada (a toll-paying highway) toward Salerno. For Vesuvius and Herculaneum, exit at Ercolano, 12km (7 miles) from Naples.

Day 1

1 ★★ kids **Vesuvius.** Vesuvius looms over much of the area covered in this guide and continues to fascinate both for its past and for what lies ahead: when will it blow? The first stop on this 3-day trip is an optional climb up to peer into the unfathomable depths of its crater. (See p 118 in Chapter 4 for details of how to visit.) There's a lot to fit into the day, and so I suggest skipping the observatory and its museum and making straight for the Quota 1000 car park, from where footpaths ascend to the crater.

Follow the road signs back down to Ercolano, and then to the Scavi di Ercolano.

Before tackling Herculaneum, you may need some lunch and there's a great little *osteria* just south of the ancient city.

2 ★★ **Osteria Viva Lo Re.** 'Long Live the King' is a contemporary osteria with a fabulous, 1,000-label

Herculaneum.

wine list and a menu that offers interesting local dishes such as pasta with octopus and artichokes, deep fried baccalà (salt cod) and ricotta and apricot soufflé. *Corso Resina 261.* ☎ *081/7390207.* *$$.*

3 ★★★ kids **Herculaneum.** The archaeological site at Herculaneum (*Ercolano* in Italian) is much more contained than Pompeii's, and

Climbing Vesuvius.

therefore easier to fit in to a short itinerary. It's no less interesting than its larger counterpart down the coast, however, and is better preserved. Make sure you have water with you; there are no refreshment facilities on site. *For a full description and practical information on Herculaneum, see p 114.*

From Herculaneum, follow the green signs back to the A3 autostrada, direction Salerno. After c. 13km (8 miles), exit the A3 at Castellmare di Stabia and follow the coast road (SP 145) to Sorrento, 48km (30 miles) south of Naples.

④ ★★ kids Sorrento. Go straight to your hotel to check in and leave your bags. You should be able to fit in a visit to the **Duomo** before an *aperitivo* in **Piazza Tasso,** followed by dinner in any of the town's fine restaurants. After dinner, wander around the grid of charming narrow lanes in the center of town and pass by the **Sedile Dominova** before heading back to the hotel for a good night's sleep.

Day 2
Sorrento's other sights can be easily covered in a morning if you start early. If you skip the out-of-the-way **Museo Correale,** you should be

able to fit in the church of **Sant' Antonino,** the charming little cloister of **San Francesco,** and the **Museobottega della Tarsialignea** before walking down to **Marina Grande** for an early lunch on the beach at **Sant'Anna Da Emilia** (see p 129) before leaving for Positano. *For a full description and practical information on Sorrento, see p 124.*

Take the torturous route over the mountain known as the Nastro Azzurro (the SP 145), which becomes increasing spectacular as you descend towards Positano.

Traffic Tip

In high season, when traffic is bad, you can leave your car in Sorrento, taking the boat to Positano and from there to Capri on Day 3. From Capri, you can return directly to Sorrento, thereby cutting down on the driving time back to Naples.

⑤ ★★★ kids Positano. This town is as short on 'sights' as it is long on spectacular views, but it's a marvelous place for wandering, window-shopping, and people-watching. Check in at your hotel and then follow the mini-tour outlined in Chapter 5, p 131, **①**, ending up on the

Sorrento's cathedral.

Soak in the evening atmosphere at Capri's Piazzetta.

Marina Grande beach for a late afternoon swim and a cold beer. *See p 139 for my pick of the town's many hotels and restaurants.*

Travel Tip

Hydrofoils ply the Positano–Capri route between April and October with the most frequent number of services running July–September. Call the tourist information office (☎ 089/875067) for a schedule.

Day 3

⑥ ★★★ **Capri.** There's no denying that Capri is magical, although in high season, the presence of thousands of day-trippers can spoil things. Ideally, you should stay overnight, but if time is limited, a day here will at least give you a taste of this most glamorous of Mediterranean islands. Catch the earliest hydrofoil possible and take the funicular railway straight up to Capri

town where you can reward yourself with a cappuccino at a bar in **Piazza Umberto I** before the hordes arrive. From here you can walk to the **Belvedere Tragara** to admire the **Faraglioni** and visit the **Certosa di San Giacomo.** *See the Capri mini-tour on p 144,* ②.

After a quick lunch, catch the bus to lower-key **Anacapri** where you should visit Axel Munthe's spectacular **Villa San Michele** and the church of San Michele. From here you can catch the chairlift up to **Monte Solaro** for all-encompassing views. If there's time, finish off the day with a trip to the **Grotta Azzurra** before catching the last hydrofoil back to the mainland.

Catch the hydrofoil back to Positano or Sorrento (depending on where you left the car) and head back to Naples via the SP 145 and A3.

The Best in **One Week**

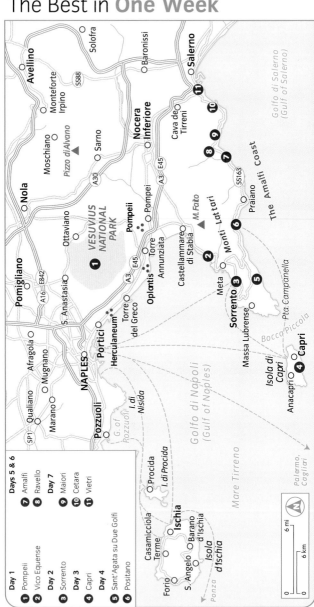

An extra four days in the area not only allows you to see more, but also to be relaxed about it. This itinerary expands on the 3-day tour giving the luxury of a night in Capri and several days to take in the Amalfi Coast tour described in Chapter 5. It starts out with a visit to the ancient city of Pompeii and finishes in Vietri, famous for its ceramics. START: **Naples.**

Head out of the city on the A3 highway towards Salerno. For Pompeii, exit at Pompeii Ovest (25km/16 miles away) and follow signs to the Scavi di Pompeii.

Day 1
❶ ★★★ kids **Pompeii.** The remains of the ancient Roman city of Pompeii are vast, and so allow a minimum of three hours, longer if you want to visit both the Villa dei Misteri and the amphitheater, which lie at opposite ends of the site. *See p 108 for a full tour of the city.*

From Pompeii, continue on the A3 towards Salerno. After c. 23km (14 miles), exit at Castellammare di Stabia and follow the coast road (SP 145) toward Sorrento, 48km (30 miles) south of Naples.

❷ ★ **Vico Equense.** Located between Castellammare and Sorrento, this picturesque town is a good place for a break. Visit the church of **Santissima Annunziata** and the **Museo Mineralogico Campano.** If you fancy a swim, there are beaches at nearby **Marina di Vico** and **Marina di Equa.** For superb homemade gelato, don't miss the famous Gelateria Gabriele at no. 5 Corso Umberto I. *See p 128.*

It's been a long day, so check into your hotel immediately. Have a look at my suggestions for making the most of your stay in Sorrento (see p 98, ❹).

Wall paintings in the Villa dei Misteri, Pompeii.

Day 2
❸ ★★ kids **Sorrento.** You have two nights and a whole day in this popular seaside resort, so you can take it easy. Beach hounds can chill out with some sunbathing and swimming; climb down the steps from the Villa Comunale public park on Piazza Tasso to the lidos where you will have to pay for a sunbed and umbrella.

On your second evening in Sorrento, I recommend dinner in one of the best restaurants in the area and a personal favorite: the Torre del Saracino at **Marina di Equa** (see p 128). It means a 15-minute drive back along the coast, but the gastronomic experience easily justifies the effort.

Day 3

No cars are allowed on Capri, so you must leave yours parked in Sorrento. Catch the hydrofoil to Capri (25 min).

4 **★★★ Capri.** You're staying the night so that you can enjoy the quiet charms of Capri once all the day-trippers have left; your hotel will send someone to meet you at the port and take care of your bags. See p 99, **6** for my suggestions for visiting the island, but add on a visit to **Emperor Tiberius's Villa Jovis** and try and fit in the spectacular circular walk that takes in the **Arco Naturale.**

Day 4

Leave Capri after breakfast and head back to Sorrento to pick up the car. Take the SP 145 from Sorrento and stop at:

5 **Sant'Agata su Due Golfi** for some fresh mountain air and a quick visit to the Renaissance church of **Santa Maria delle Grazie** with its inlaid marble altar.

From Sant'Agata, a spectacular 14km (8¹/₂-mile) drive brings you to:

6 **★★★ kids Positano.** You will arrive in time to check into your hotel, have a bite to eat, and look around the town before a leisurely dinner (see p 98, **5**).

For detailed coverage of sights, hotels, and restaurants in Positano, see p 131.

Days 5 & 6

Make an early start because there's lots to see today. You can read more about the sights and restaurants on the classic Amalfi Coast drive on p 130 of Chapter 5. Worthwhile stop-offs along the winding coast road from Positano include **Praiano, Marina di Praia** (where I recommend lunch on the beach at **Alfonso a Mare,** see p 139), **Marina di Furore,** and the **Grotta dello Smeraldo.** And don't miss **Conca dei Marini.**

There should be time when you've checked into your hotel in Amalfi to fit in some sightseeing before dinner.

7 **★★ kids Amalfi.** For a mini-tour of Amalfi, see p 135, **8**. On your walk around the colorful little town, you can take in the grandiose **Duomo,** the **Museo della Carta,** and the atmospheric medieval streets such as the **Ruga Nova Mercatorum.** Be sure to make time for coffee and a delicious local pastry at **Café Pansa** in Piazza del Duomo (☎ 089/871065). *For*

Ravello's cathedral has two magnificent pulpits.

Evening in the Piazzetta, Capri Town.

detailed coverage of sights, hotels, and restaurants in Amalfi, see p 130.

Just out of Amalfi on the road to Ravello, you pass charming little Atrani, which is worth a short visit.

8 ★★★ **Ravello.** The winding road up to Ravello branches off the main coastal road just after Atrani. You will arrive in this captivating town around lunchtime, and so after finding your hotel and something to eat, there should be plenty of time to see the **Duomo,** the little church of **San Giovanni del Toro,** and **Villa Rufolo.**

Wherever you end up eating and staying, do stop off at a bar at **Piazza Duomo** for an after-dinner coffee or *digestivo*. The square, with it is marble sidewalk, lovely old buildings, and soft light, is magical at night. *For detailed coverage of sights, hotels, and restaurants in Ravello, see p 140.*

Day 7
Start the last day of this tour with a visit to the gardens of Ravello's **Villa Cimbrone** and then head back down to the madness of the coast road and continue the drive east. You could stop off for a swim at the long beach in **9** **Maiori** before continuing to the delightful fishing port town of **10** **Cetara,** famous for its bottled anchovies and *colatura di alici*, a kind of anchovy sauce. Back on the road, the last Amalfi Coast stop is **11** **Vietri** where you can purchase some of the colorful ceramics for which the town is so famous.

Head back to Naples on the A3 (about 50km/31 miles) autostrada, which you can pick up at Vietri.

Cetara.

The Best in **Ten Days**

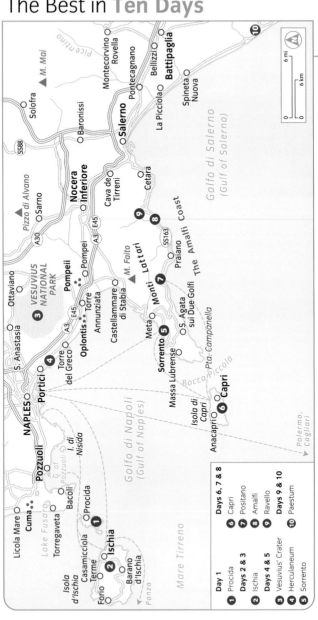

Day 1
1. Procida

Days 2 & 3
2. Ischia

Days 4 & 5
3. Vesuvius' Crater
4. Herculaneum
5. Sorrento

Days 6, 7 & 8
6. Capri
7. Positano
8. Amalfi

Days 9 & 10
9. Ravello
10. Paestum

The middle part of this tour is identical to 'The Best in One Week' (see p 100), but I suggest a trip to the islands of Procida and Ischia rather than Capri at the beginning and a visit to the majestic Doric temples of Paestum at the end. START: Naples.

Procida's Ciracciello beach.

From Naples, Procida is a 40-minute ride on the car ferry.

Day 1
❶ ★★ kids **Procida.** There could be no better respite from the chaos and noise of Naples than the laid-back little island of Procida. You can easily while away a day here visiting the **Castello d'Avalos** and the **Terra Mutata,** buzzy **Marina Grande,** and charming, sleepy **Corricella.** It also has the best beaches of all the islands and there are some excellent restaurants. *For detailed coverage of sights, hotels, and restaurants on Procida, see p 158.*

From Procida, catch one of the regular car ferries to Ischia; journey time is about 25 minutes.

Days 2 & 3
❷ ★★★ kids **Ischia.** Big enough to warrant a 2-night stopover, Ischia is all about wellbeing, so you may choose to spend your time here wallowing in its famed thermal

waters. However, there are also some interesting sights. Sun worshippers have no shortage of beaches to choose from and gourmets will appreciate the great choice of restaurants on the island. *For detailed coverage of sights, hotels, and restaurants on Ischia, see p 150.*

From Ischia, catch the boat back to Naples (1 hr). Then follow the signs to the A3 autostrada; direction Salerno. After 12km (7 miles) exit at Ercolano for both Vesuvius and Herculaneum.

Days 4 & 5
Leave Ischia as early as possible; before arriving in Sorrento, you have visits planned to ❸ **Vesuvius' Crater** and ❹ **Herculaneum.** See 'The Best in Three Days', Day 1, p 96, for this part of the tour.

Continue south on the A3, exiting at Castellammare di Stabia; follow the coast road (SP 145) for 20km (12 miles) to Sorrento.

Ischia Ponte.

Arrive in **⑤ Sorrento** in time to find your hotel and enjoy an *aperitivo* before dinner and bed; tomorrow is for sightseeing. *For detailed coverage of sights, hotels, and restaurants in Sorrento, see p 124.*

Days 6, 7 & 8
Visit **⑥ Capri, ⑦ Positano, ⑧ Amalfi,** and **⑨ Ravello.** See 'The Best in One Week', Days 5 to 7, p 102, for this part of the tour.

Days 9 & 10
Leave Ravello early because you may want to stop in Atrani, Cetara, or Vietri before heading south to Paestum. See Day 7 in 'The Best in One Week,' p 103, for more on these places.

From Vietri, pass through Salerno to join the southbound coast road (SP 175) that takes you to Paestum, 42km (26 miles) away.

Overnight at Paestum

You're staying the night near the Paestum archeological site, and so even if there's no time for a full visit when you arrive, make sure you at least get a view of the temples after dark when they're floodlit. The road passes nearby. An overnight stay at the Azienda Agricola Seliano offers comfortable accommodation and delicious home-cooked food on a working farm, only 3¼km (2 miles) from the temples (off the main road from Paestum to Capaccio Scalo). The farm produce includes fresh mozzarella. *Via Seliano, Paestum.* ☎ *0828/723634. www.agrituris moseliano.it. 9 units. Doubles 75–120€. MC, V.*

⑩ ★★ kids Paestum. Spend the morning marveling at the majestic Doric temples that were once part of the Greek city of Paestum. Be sure to leave time for a visit to the museum, and if the timing works, drop by the temples at sunset to see the three giants at their most romantic. *For a full description and tour of the archaeological site, see p 120.*

Head back to Naples (if that's where you're going) via the northbound SS 18, picking up the A3 westbound at Battipaglia. ●

Pompeii

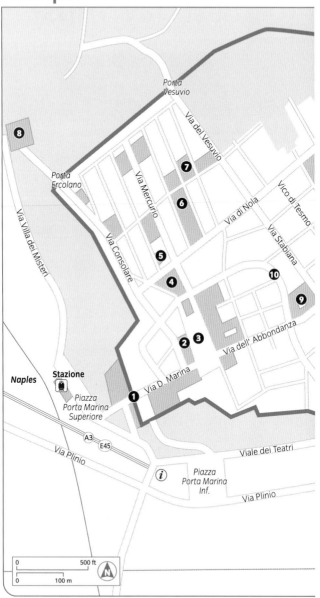

Porta
Vesuvio

Via del Vesuvio

Porta
Ercolano

Via Mercurio

Via di Nola

Vico di Tesmo

Via Stabiana

Via Consolare

Via Villa dei Misteri

Via dell' Abbondanza

Naples

Stazione

Piazza
Porta Marina
Superiore

Via D. Marina

A3 E45

Via Plinio

Viale dei Teatri

Piazza
Porta Marina
Inf.

Via Plinio

0   500 ft
0   100 m

Previous page: Il Foro, Pompeii.

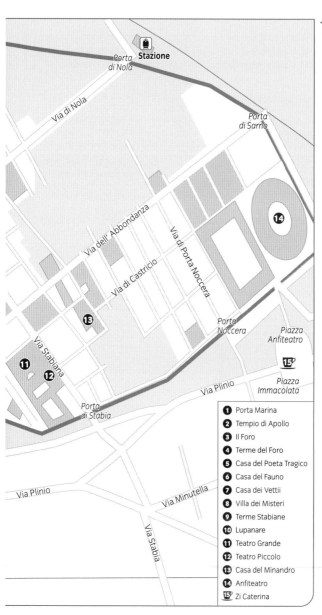

1 Porta Marina
2 Tempio di Apollo
3 Il Foro
4 Terme del Foro
5 Casa del Poeta Tragico
6 Casa del Fauno
7 Casa dei Vettii
8 Villa dei Misteri
9 Terme Stabiane
10 Lupanare
11 Teatro Grande
12 Teatro Piccolo
13 Casa del Minandro
14 Anfiteatro
15 Zi Caterina

Probably founded in the 7th century B.C., the city of Pompeii was once home to 20,000 souls. A cosmopolitan commercial center laid out in a typical grid pattern, it was a popular ritzy holiday spot among Roman patricians who built grand villas and enjoyed the town's brothels and spas. START: **Porta Marina, 23km (14¹/₂ miles) from Naples. Trip length: three hours minimum.**

Preparing for your visit

There is very little shade at Pompeii, so wear a hat, bring sun block if you come in the summer, and make sure you have plenty of water (there are no bars on-site). Good solid shoes are essential at any time of the year.

1 Porta Marina. Although there is also a ticket office at Piazza Anfiteatro, this tour begins at Porta Marina, the principal entrance to the city, which was once accessible from the sea. There is also a bookshop and a booth distributing audio guides, which I would recommend hiring to help make sense of the enormous site.

2 ★ Tempio di Apollo. Dating from c. 575 B.C., the Temple to Apollo stands on the western side of the Forum and is among the

Pompeii.

oldest structures in the city. On either side of the portico are statues of Apollo and Diana depicted as archers (the originals are in the Archaeological Museum in Naples).

3 ★★ Il Foro. A huge, rectangular grassy space located at the intersection of the city's two main streets, the Forum was Pompeii's main square and the center of civic life. No cart traffic was allowed and it was surrounded on all sides by important religious, political, and commercial buildings, such as the temples of Jupiter and Apollo, and the *macellum*, the covered meat and fish market.

4 ★ Terme del Foro. Public baths (*terme*) were an extremely important part of Roman life, and there were several in Pompeii. These smallish baths date from after 80 B.C. and typically include separate sections for men and women, each of which was laid out in the following sequence: *apodyterium* (changing room), *frigidarium* (cold bathing room), *tepidarium* (warm room), and *caldarium* (hot room). Delicate stucco decorations have survived here.

Taking a Break?

At the time of writing, there were no refreshments available within the site. There are plenty of bars and cafés near each of the entrances/exits, however, so buy a sandwich and something to drink and find a quiet spot for a picnic during your tour.

5 ★ Casa del Poeta Tragico.
The typical 'atrium style' House of the Tragic Poet is famous for the black and white mosaic of a chained, fierce-looking dog in the doorway with the inscription *Cave Canem* (Beware of the Dog).

6 ★★★ Casa del Fauno. This 2nd century B.C. house (named after the delicate bronze statue of a faun in the impluvium) was one of the city's largest and most sophisticated dwellings. Unusually, it is built round two porticoed atria between which lie the exedra, the discussion hall, and heart of the house. The million-piece mosaic depicting the battle of Issus was found here; it is now in the Archeological Museum in Naples, along with the original statue of the faun.

7 ★★★ Casa dei Vettii. Two blocks to the east is this wealthy merchant's house, which contains some extraordinarily well-preserved wall paintings, the most infamous being the well-endowed figure of Priapus, god of fertility, in the doorway. Through the atrium on the right of the entrance is the kitchen, complete with cooking pots placed on a hearth. Off the kitchen is a small room decorated with erotic wall paintings and a statue-fountain of Priapus. No prizes for guessing where the water spouted. The sitting room is famous for its magnificent

House of the Faun.

wall paintings in 'Pompeiian Red'. This house has been closed for restoration work for some years; it is hoped it will reopen during 2010.

8 ★★★ Villa dei Misteri. Outside the Porta Ercolano (at the north west corner of the site) is this large country house, the most famous of all Pompeii's buildings, which contains the city's best-preserved frescoes. Among these is the celebrated cycle of paintings that illustrates a young girl's initiation into the forbidden cult of Dionysus, against a background of vivid Pompeiian red.

9 ★★★ Terme Stabiane. Back within the walls, head toward the southern end of the site and this, the

The Forum with Vesuvius looming in the background.

oldest and most complete bath complex in Pompeii, once heated by underground furnaces. Look out for the delicate stucco decorations on the walls of the open, rectangular palestra. The complex houses two cases containing plaster casts of the dead, unearthed during 19th century excavations nearby. When human remains were found, plaster was poured into the moulds left by their rotted bodies in the solidified ash, resulting in disturbing casts of terrified humans frozen in time. These *terme* were closed for structural work at the time of writing and are unlikely to reopen before late 2010.

⓾ ★ Lupanare. Situated just north of the *terme*, this was the city's only purpose-built brothel (*Lupa* means she wolf and prostitute in Latin). A series of small rooms contain stone beds where mattresses were laid, while paintings illustrate various positions that were used in the erotic games designed to titillate the customers.

⓫ ★ Teatro Grande. At the southern limit of the city is the theater complex. The Large Theater, with its spectacular natural backdrop of the Monti Lattari, was built in the 2nd century B.C. and could seat 5,000 spectators. It was linked to the Forum by the

Terme Stabiane.

bustling, shop-lined main thoroughfare, Via dell'Abbondanza.

⓬ ★★ Teatro Piccolo. Sometimes called the Odeum, the beautiful Small Theater was built a hundred or so years after the Large Theater. Seating 1,000, it is much better preserved than its larger counterpart and probably had a roof to ensure good acoustics.

⓭ ★★ Casa del Minandro. Named after the Greek poet Menander, this huge patrician's villa was restored recently and features vivid wall paintings, a small private bath complex, and a porticoed garden atrium.

⓮ ★★ Anfiteatro. Some 20,000 citizens could fit into Pompeii's 70 B.C. amphitheater which is one of the oldest and best-preserved of its kind in existence and would have been used principally for gladiator fights.

⓯ ★ kids Zi Caterina. This pleasant restaurant, with its menu of seafood dishes and pizza, is next to the Piazza del Anfiteatro entrance to the site, and so perfectly situated for a post-visit bite. Try the local Lacrima Cristi wine. *Via Roma 20.* ☎ *081/8507447. $–$$.*

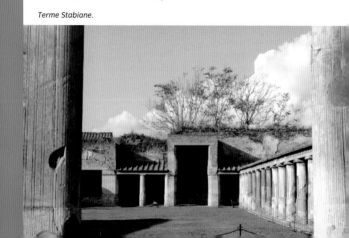

Fresco detail, Villa dei Misteri, Pompeii.

Scavi di Pompeii, Porta Marina, Via Villa dei Misteri 2. ☎ 081/8575347. www.pompeiisites.org. Admission 11€ adults, 5.50€ EU citizens 18–24 yrs, free EU citizens under 18 or over 65. Nov–Mar daily 8:30am–5pm (last entrance 3:30pm), Apr–Oct daily 8:30am–7:30pm (last entrance 6pm). Closed 1 Jan, 1 May, 25 Dec. Visit in late afternoon to avoid the crowds. Circumvesuviana railway from Naples (Naples–Sorrento line) to Pompeii Scavi-Villa dei Misteri (journey time 30 min).

A City Suspended in Time

On the morning of August 24 A.D. 79, Vesuvius erupted with devastating effect; lying directly in its path to the south-east, Pompeii was totally consumed by stones and ash. A fair number of Pompeiians had probably fled by the time the fireworks started, but what was left behind has given us extraordinary insight into the life of a thriving Roman city, thanks to the painstaking work of generations of archaeologists who carried out the first excavations in 1748. Suspended in time, Pompeii today is a poignant ghost town, which you can coax into life with a little imagination. Wandering the streets, spot the grooves worn in the paving by heavy carts, cross the roads on the huge stepping stones designed to keep feet dry when it rained, read graffiti on walls, peek into the baker's shop where bread ovens are still standing, and admire the wall-paintings that adorned ancient living rooms.

Herculaneum

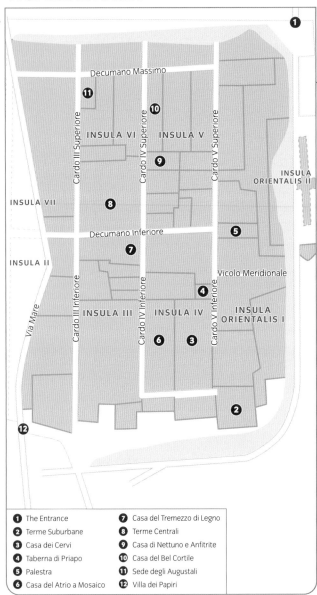

1 The Entrance
2 Terme Suburbane
3 Casa dei Cervi
4 Taberna di Priapo
5 Palestra
6 Casa del Atrio a Mosaico
7 Casa del Tremezzo di Legno
8 Terme Centrali
9 Casa di Nettuno e Anfitrite
10 Casa del Bel Cortile
11 Sede degli Augustali
12 Villa dei Papiri

Situated just inland on the southwest side of Vesuvius, the exclusive town of Herculaneum was probably founded in the 4th century b.c., although most of what is visible today dates from the 2nd century b.c. Compared to Pompeii, the site is small although you can see only part of the whole town; the rest remains buried beneath the modern town of Ercolano. **START: site entrance, 10-minute walk downhill from Ercolano–Scavi station. Trip length: 12 km ((8 miles).**

An overview of Herculaneum.

❶ ★ The Entrance. The access ramp gives you a good overview of the Roman town, lying 30m (100 ft) below modern street level. Look how threateningly close Vesuvius looms behind. After the ticket office, the ramp curves around the southern end of the site leading to the booth where you can purchase an audio guide (which I recommend) and a bookshop. From here, take the metal ramp that leads down through a tunnel in the solid rock, emerging at the ancient shoreline. The arched *fornici* facing you were used as storerooms or boat houses. Around 300 human skeletons were discovered here in the 1980s, together with items of jewelry and coins, keys to houses, and work tools; the poor souls, having grabbed their most valuable assets, were probably waiting to be rescued by sea when the lethal spew from the volcano hit.

❷ ★ Terme Suburbane. Above the *fornici* is the large terrace where

senator Marcus Nonius Balbus's monument stands, and the entrance to the large Suburban Bath complex (usually open only in the mornings), among the best-preserved examples of its kind in antiquity and built outside the old city walls.

Refreshments . . . or lack of them

There is a bar within the site at Herculaneum, but it was closed at the time of writing with no sign of reopening. There are a few booths selling hot and cold drinks, sandwiches, and ice cream, near the car park, but be sure to bring bottled water.

❸ ★★ Casa dei Cervi. Up the ramp from the baths lies the Casa dei Cervi (the House of the Deer), one of the grandest villas of the ancient city. The house is named after the two statues (copies) of deer being

Casa dei Cervi.

attacked by dogs that stand in the lovely garden, which once over-looked the sea; the big terrace at the front must have had marvelous views over the Bay of Naples. The house boasts some striking black and red wall decorations.

④ Taberna di Priapo. To the north, on the left hand corner, is Pria-pus's Tavern with its waiting room at the back (for customers requiring more than just food and drink) and, next door, a *thermopolium*, the ancient equivalent of a fast food joint complete with amphorae to keep food warm set into marble counters.

⑤ ★ Palestra. Across the road is the columned entrance to the town's large Palestra, dating from the Augustinian era (27 B.C.–A.D. 14), where the Romans passed their lei-sure time playing ball games and wrestling. Laid out over two ter-races and with a long colonnade, it has only been partially excavated.

⑥ ★ Casa del Atrio a Mosaico. Towards the bottom of Cardo IV is this huge, once-luxurious villa with a geometrically-patterned mosaic pavement in the atrium.

⑦ ★★ Casa del Tremezzo di Legno. At the intersection with the Decumano Inferiore is the large house named after the partially

carbonized wooden partition sepa-rating the atrium garden from the *tablinum* (study).

⑧ ★★★ Terme Centrali. Across the Decumano Inferiore is the entrance to the women's section of the Central Baths; the men's section is accessible across the grassy, col-onnaded palestra but also has its own entrance on the Cardo III. Look out for the changing rooms with shelves for depositing togas and other belongings, fabulous black and white mosaic pavements (those

Moasic floor in the women's section of the Terme Centrali.

in the women's section are particularly well-preserved), the round *frigidarium* (for cold-water bathing) decorated with paintings of fish, and the next door *caldarium* with its tub for hot water baths.

⑨ ★★★ Casa di Nettuno e Anfitrite. Farther up the Cardo IV, just past the *Bottega* (a shop with amphora-stacked shelves), is this house named after Neptune and Aphrodite, the subjects of the bright blue mosaic in the *nymphaeum* (shrine) at the rear.

⑩ ★ Casa del Bel Cortile. This house, on two levels, indeed has a 'Lovely Courtyard'. In the main room is a glass case containing the skeletons of a 15 year-old boy and a young man and women, all found on the beach.

⑪ ★★ Sede degli Augustali. At the top-left corner of the site is this imposing public building, once the administrative headquarters of an organization dedicated to the cult of emperors and named after the Emperor Augustus. In the far room are two vivid wall paintings; the one on the left shows Hercules arriving in Olympia after his labors accompanied by Juno, Minerva, and Jupiter.

⑫ ★★★ Villa dei Papiri. Among Herculaneum's most famous buildings, this villa actually lies outside the main site but has been closed since 2007 for restoration work; 'they' say that it will probably reopen within 2010. The once luxurious villa is named after the 1,000-odd badly charred but legible papyrus scrolls that were discovered here. The other extraordinary treasures revealed during excavations were nearly 90 sculptures, in both marble and bronze (Roman copies of Greek originals). These magnificent works are now housed in Rooms 114–117 of the Museo Archeologico in Naples (see p 31, ⑫).

Scavi di Ercolano. Corso Resina 1, Ercolano. ☎ 081/7324311, 081/7777008. www.pompeiisites.org. Admission 11€ adults, 5.50€ EU citizens 18–24 yrs, free EU citizens under 18 or over 65. Nov–Mar daily 8:30am–5pm (last entrance 3:30pm), Apr–Oct daily 8:30am–7:30pm (last entrance 6pm). Closed 1 Jan, 1 May, 25 Dec. Circumvesuviana train from Naples to Ercolano–Scavi station (journey time 17 min).

The Angry Mountain

When Vesuvius erupted on August 24, A.D. 79, the town of Herculaneum and its 5,000 inhabitants were engulfed in clouds of burning, noxious pyroclastic material whose extreme heat caused instant death and buried buildings under a 30-m (100-ft) layer of volcanic mud. The particular quality of this mud is responsible for the remarkable degree of preservation found here; in contrast to the ash and pumice that rained down on Pompeii, this substance quickly solidified and created a seal, which left buildings (including, in many cases, their upper floors) and even organic material intact. The result is an extraordinarily vivid time capsule, less famous than Pompeii maybe, but more alive.

Vesuvius

- **1** Museo dell'Osservatorio
- **2** Quota 1000
- **3** The Crater
- **4** Bar

You can't miss Vesuvius. Standing at around 1,280m (4,266 ft) high just east of Naples, its truncated cone shape looms over the city, the bay, and the islands, omnipresent. The volcano has fascinated visitors for centuries and these days, around 400,000 people climb up to its rim every year. The area is now a national park and a UNESCO Biosphere Reserve. **START: Either at the Observatory or at the car park at Quota 1000.**

Getting There

Catch the Circumvesuviana train to Ercolano-Scavi from where the Vesuvius shuttle bus takes you up to the car park at Quota 1000, stopping at the Observatory on the way.

1 ★ **Museo dell'Osservatorio.** Halfway up the mountainside lies the original Bourbon-era observatory and its small museum documenting the history of the scientific research

concerned with the volcano and the threat that it poses. Amazingly, this building has survived the past seven eruptions. ⏱ *30 min. Via Osservatorio.* ☎ *081/6108438. Free admission. Sat & Sun 10am–2pm.*

2 **Quota 1000.** Vehicles can go no farther than this point (which lies at 1,000m (3,330 ft) above sea level), where the bus stops and there is a car park. From here, the 121m (400 ft) climb up to the crater

Blowing its Top

It's a question of when and not if: mainland Europe's only active volcano *will* erupt again. Vesuvius last blew its top in 1944 and the longer it lies dormant, the greater the risk of an eruption. Its inner rumblings have been monitored by the Osservatorio Vesuviano since 1841 and evacuation plans will be activated at the first sign of trouble. However, when you look at the lower slopes of the mountain and see how densely populated it is (around 1,000,000 people live in the 'comuni vesuviani'), you realize how critical the situation could be. Experts believe that a present-day eruption will be similar to that of A.D. 79: A surge cloud will flow down the mountain at 65–80 kph (40–50 mph) reaching a temperature of around 400°C (752°F). Anyone in its path will be carbonized.

rim along a well-kept path takes around half an hour. *2€ parking.*

Travel Tip

The best time to make the ascent is early in the morning. Wear good, solid shoes, and carry water and sunscreen. The crater is closed in bad or very windy weather.

3 ★★★ The Crater. You must pay to approach the rim of the crater, but once up close, you get to peer down into its fascinating, unknown depths. Of course, the other reason to be up here is to admire the peerless views,

which on a clear day encompass Naples and the bay, the Sorrentine Peninsula, and the islands. *⏱ 1 hour for the return journey from Quota 1000. ☎ 081/7710939. www.parco nazionaledelvesuvio.it/grancono. Admission 6.50€ adults, 4.50€ 8–18 yrs, free under-8s. Daily 9am–2 hrs before sunset.*

4 Bar. The only place to buy refreshments is located at Quota 1000. The bar is nothing special, but you can relax with a cold drink and a sandwich and enjoy the view. *Quota 1000, Parco Nazionale di Vesuvio. No phone. $.*

Vesuvius: you can't get away from it.

Paestum

The ancient city of Poseidonia was probably founded around 600 B.C. by Sybaritic Greeks. The town flourished and three great Doric temples were built in the 5th–4th centuries B.C. When the Romans colonized in 273 B.C., they renamed it Paestum and added a forum and amphitheater. These are some of the best-preserved buildings of their kind outside Greece. START: **Porta Giudizia. Trip length: three hours.**

Public Transport

Trains run from Naples to Paestum station (journey ⏲ ca. 1½ hour) from where it's a 10-minute walk to the archaeological site. Regular bus services from Salerno train station are run by CSTP (☎ 800 016659; www.cstp.it).

☕ Bar Anna. With its pleasant terrace, this is a good place for a pre-visit drink, snack, or ice cream. *Via Magna Grecia.* ☎ *0828/811196. $.*

❷ Porta Giustizia. The site has two entrances; this itinerary starts at Porta Giudizia to the south. The first sight of three temples rising above the low-lying site and surrounded by fields and wild flowers, is unforgettable.

❸ Via Sacra. The dead-straight road running north–south through the middle of the site is known as the 'Sacred Road,' where processions were held. The Romans called it the *cardus maximus* but it is, in fact, Greek in origin.

in around 550 B.C., it is the earliest of the three temples.

5 ★★★ Tempio di Nettuno.

The jewel of the site is this magnificent construction, the best preserved and largest of the three temples, possibly dedicated to Poseidon or, according to a more recent theory, Apollo. It was built in around 450 B.C and is amazingly intact; only the roof and internal walls are missing. Like the other temples, it was constructed using local limestone rather than marble.

6 ★ Forum.

The forum was the hub of any Roman city; this one was enclosed on four sides by a covered colonnade with taverns and shops. On the northern side, there was a sports and leisure complex, which included a rectangular *piscina* (pool) with a labyrinth for underwater swimming.

7 ★ Ekklesiasterion.

This survivor of the Greek city, once part of the *agorà*, was an open air theater, a circular construction with tiered

Tomb of the Diver, Museo Archeologico Nazionale.

4 ★★★ Basilica (Tempio di Hera).

The archaeologists who first discovered the city of Paestum in the 18th century mistook this building for a basilica, but we now know that it was constructed as a temple to Hera (Juno), the wife of Zeus. Built

Tempio di Nettuno at night.

seating. It was probably used for important meetings of the city council.

❽ ★ Anfiteatro. Next to the ekklesiasterion is the amphitheater, begun during the 1st century B.C. but later enlarged to provide seating for around 2,000. At least half the construction lies under the road that cuts through the city.

❾ ★★ Tempio di Cerere. The third and smallest of the temples is now thought to have been dedicated to the goddess Athena rather than to Ceres, the goddess of fertility. The temple was used as an early Christian burial site and as a church in medieval times.

❿ ★★★ Museo Archeologico Nazionale di Paestum. This wonderful museum houses architectural fragments and other relics of the town together with finds from the sanctuary of Hera Argiva, a recently unearthed Greek site at the mouth of the river Sele. The most important pieces are on the first floor and include a 5th-century-B.C. marble statue of Hera, a 6th-century-B.C. female bust in painted terracotta, a collection of 5th-century-B.C. sculptured *metopes* (decorative elements) from the temples, a statue of Zeus in terracotta, and a bronze statue of Sileno Marsia.

The star turn is the fabulous collection of 3rd- to 5th-century-B.C. tomb paintings, the most famous of which is the almost perfectly preserved Tomb of the Diver, a superb example of a 'painted box tomb', which was unearthed as recently as 1968. The four lateral slabs are decorated with banqueting scenes; the 5th (the cover) depicts a marvelous image of a graceful young diver in full flight, about to slice into the water. The haunting scene is thought to symbolize the passage from life to the world of the dead.

Statue of Hera in Paestum's Museo Archeologico Nazionale.

⓫ Fattoria del Casaro. A 10-minute walk from Porta Giustizia brings you to this farm that makes its own mozzarella di bufala. There's a restaurant serving rustic local food, or they will make you up a sandwich. *Via Licinella 5.* ☎ *0828/722704. $–$$.*

Via Magna Grecia 919. ☎ *0828/811023. www.infopaestum.it. Museum only: Admission 4€ adults, 2€ 18–25 yrs; museum plus archaeological site: 6.50€ adults, 3.25€ 18–25 yrs; free admission under 18s and over 65s. Visit in late afternoon to avoid crowds and catch the evening light. Daily 9am–1 hr. before sunset; museum daily 9am–7pm. Closed 1st, 3rd, & 5th Mon of month.*

Travel Tip

Ask about the Summer program of night time visits to Paestum; the sight of the temples lit by moonlight is truly magical: ☎ 0828/811023 for information. ●

5 Best **Islands & Towns on the Amalfi Coast**

Sorrento

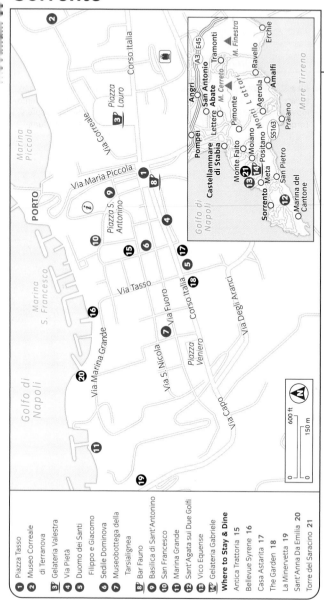

Previous page: Positano from the terrace of the Hotel San Pietro.

Sorrento is set on top of sheer cliffs overlooking the Bay of Naples, from the northern shore of the jutting Sorrentine Peninsula. The area has been settled since prehistoric times with Etruscans, Greeks, and Romans all moving in. Although modern Sorrento has lost much of its Grand Tour luster, it's still a very popular resort and makes a good base for touring. START: **Piazza Tasso.**

1 ★ kids **Piazza Tasso.** This busy square is named after Sorrento's most famous literary son, the poet Torquato Tasso (1544–95); there's a statue of him next to Bar Fauno. With its central location, the square is usually a-buzz with traffic and people, its pavement cafés popular for a morning cappuccino or an evening *aperitivo*. On the north side of the piazza there's a balcony overlooking a deep gully that leads to **Marina Piccola** where the ferries to and from Naples, Capri, and the other coastal towns dock. To the right is the entrance to Sorrento's grandest of grand hotels, the Grand Hotel Vittoria where the great tenor Enrico Caruso once stayed. You can usually pop in and have a look at its glorious garden without being harassed by hotel staff. ⏱ *45 min. Piazza Tasso.*

2 ★ **Museo Correale di Terranova.** Housed in the grand 18th-century villa of the Counts of Terranova, who left their home and its contents to the town of Sorrento in the 1920s, this museum displays their collection of paintings, furniture, and the decorative arts plus local archaeological finds. Particularly interesting is the collection of 18th-century Italian and European porcelain originating in such factories as Capodimonte, Doccia, Meissen, Frankenthal, and Chelsea. The lovely garden offers fine views of the bay. ⏱ *1 hr. Via Correale 50.* ☎ *081/8781846. www.sorrento-online.com/museocorreale. Admission 6€, 3€ under-12s. Wed–Mon 9am–2pm.*

3 ★★ **Gelateria Valestra.** On the way back into the center of town, stop off at this farm shop, which sells superb homemade ice cream (try the sinful zabaglione) as well as home-produced cheeses. *Piazza Angelina Lauro 45.* ☎ *081/8785784. $.*

Piazza Tasso, Sorrento.

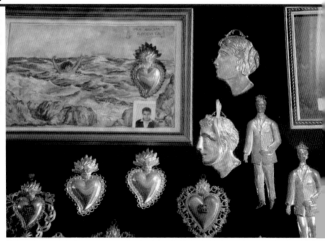

Sant'Antonino: the sailor's friend.

4 Via Pietà. From just behind Torquato Tasso's statue in Piazza Tasso, narrow Via Pietà leads west, passing several imposing palazzi. At no. 18, the 14th-century **Palazzo Correale** was built in Catalan style but has a splendid rococo majolica courtyard (the 'Esedra Maiolica'), reminiscent of the cloister at Santa Chiara in Naples. The building is privately owned, but the courtyard is occupied by a florist's shop from

Card players at the Sedile Dominova.

where you can see the trompe l'oeil back wall. At no. 14, 13th-century **Palazzo Veniero** has windows framed with arches in patterned brick and no. 24, just before the arch at the end of the street, has Gothic arched windows. ⏱ *10 min.*

5 ★ Duomo dei Santi Filippo e Giacomo. This site was once occupied by a Romanesque cathedral, but was rebuilt in the 15th century. What you see today is relatively modern although a few old features have survived such as the 16th-century Bishop's marble throne. The nave is divided by solid columns supporting rounded arches and the side chapels are decorated with 16th- and 17th-century paintings. The choir stalls feature local wood intarsia work and there's a magnificent organ loft (look up as you leave the building). ⏱ *30 min. Corso Italia/Via Giuliani.* ☎ *081/ 8782248. Free admission. Daily 7.45am–noon & 4.30–8.30pm.*

6 ★ Sedile Dominova. Situated at the heart of Sorrento's old town, this place must be a strong contender for the prize for most picturesque working men's club just about anywhere. It was also a meeting place in the 15th century, but a little more upscale: aristocratic bigwigs would get together among the now faded frescoes of this open loggia to discuss local politics. These days, the place is popular with old-timers playing cards, although they're probably discussing local politics too. ⏱ *5 min. Via San Cesario/Via Giuliani.*

7 ★★ **Museobottega della Tarsialignea.** More local intarsia work is on display in this museum, housed in red-painted **Palazzo Pomarici Santomasi.** Sorrento artisans became famous for this type of wood marquetry in the mid-1700s, and the museum contains a wonderful collection of furniture and objects illustrating the intricate craft. You can buy examples of contemporary artisans' work in the museum shop and visit them at work in two 'botteghe' (workshops) next door. ⏱ *1 hr. Via San Nicola 28.* ☎ *081/ 8771942. www.alessandrofiorentino collection.it. Admission 8€ adults, 5€ over 60s and 12–18 yrs, free under-12s. Oct–May Tues–Sun 10am–1pm & 3–6:30pm, June–Sep Tues–Sun 10am–1pm & 4–7:30pm.*

8 ★★ **Bar Fauno.** This elegant café with its large pavement terrace is a good place for a light lunch. Choose from giant salads, pasta dishes, and toasted sandwiches; good pre-dinner cocktails too. *Piazza Tasso 13–15.* ☎ *081/8787735. $–$$.*

9 ★ **Basilica di Sant'Antonino.** This rather odd-looking baroque church, dedicated to the town's patron saint, stands on the site of a much earlier church; the 11th-century wood door dates from the original building. Sant'Antonino, the protector of sailors, is said to have saved a small child who had been swallowed by a whale; hence, the whalebone mounted on the wall of the porch. It's lovely inside with a coffered ceiling and ranks of chandeliers. Two staircases lead down to the marble crypt displaying ex-votos from shipwrecked sailors and paintings of boats in heavy seas. The saint's tomb is down here too. ⏱ *15 min. Piazza Sant'Antonino. No phone. Free admission. Daily 9am–noon & 5–7pm.*

10 ★★★ **San Francesco.** Via San Francesco leads north to this little

San Francesco's pretty cloister.

Fishing fleet at Marina Grande.

both pointed and rounded arches and octagonal columns with carved capitals. It encloses a pretty garden with roses and wisteria, an enchanting setting for the concerts, exhibitions, and weddings that are held here. ⏱ *15 min. Via San Francesco.* ☎ *081/8781269. Free admission. Daily 8am–10pm.*

⓫ ★★★ kids Marina Grande. In spite of its name, picturesque Marina Grande, Sorrento's original fishing harbor, is actually smaller than Marina Piccola and has managed to retain a more genuine atmosphere than the rest of this elegant town. Accessed by steep steps leading down from Via Marina Grande, the muddle of dilapidated buildings is strung out along the beach and quayside where kids play football, fishermen mend their nets, and stray dogs and cats doze in the sun. There are a couple of decent restaurants down here too (see p 129).

church and its adorable 14th-century cloister. Forget the church, but don't miss the so-called **Chiostro del Paradiso** to the left, which features

Around Sorrento

If you want to leave the crowds behind, head to the hilly interior of the Sorrentine Peninsula, an area rich in unparalleled natural scenery from where the land dips away to sheer southern coastline in a head-spinning way. **⓬ Sant'Agata sui Due Golfi** lies 390m (1,300 ft) up; apart from the views, you can admire the magnificent inlaid altar in the Renaissance church of **Santa Maria delle Grazie** and splash out on a meal at one of Italy's best-known restaurants, Don Alfonso 1890. From here, the famous **Nastro Azzurro** (Blue Ribbon) road wends its spectacular, 14km (8½ miles) way down to Positano. Back down on the coast and just east of Sorrento, picturesque **⓭ Vico Equense** makes a low-key alternative to Sorrento as a base for exploring. Among the town's sights is the 14th-century church of **Santissima Annunziata,** built dramatically on the top of sheer cliffs. Gelato-holics shouldn't miss the artisan ice cream at **⓮ Gelateria Gabriele at Corso Umberto I 5.** If you feel like a swim, there's a good beach near **Marina di Equa,** a picturesque seaside village dominated by a Saracen watchtower and home to my favorite restaurant in the whole region, the Torre del Saracino (see p 129).

Where to **Stay & Dine**

★★ **Antica Trattoria** *MODERN ITALIAN* Among Sorrento's best restaurants, dishes such as risotto with sea bass and duck breast with artichoke hearts are served here on a lovely, flower-filled terrace. *Via P. Reginaldo Giuliani 33.* ☎ *081/8071082. www.lanticatrattoria.com. Entrees 23–29€. AE, DC, MC, V. Lunch & dinner daily. Map p 124.*

★★★ **Bellevue Syrene** Dating from 1826, this hotel has antiques, grand mirrors, and original moldings that coexist with contemporary furniture and art. Views are fabulous and there's a private beach. *Piazza della Vittoria 5.* ☎ *081/8781024. www.bellevue.it. 48 units. Doubles 250–550€ w/breakfast. AE, DC, MC, V. Map p 124.*

★ **Casa Astarita** This small B&B offers bright, modern rooms, tiled bathrooms and the cozy atmosphere of a private home. Breakfast, with homemade cakes, is delicious. *Corso Italia 67.* ☎ *081/8774906. www.casastarita.com. 6 units. Doubles 70–110€ w/breakfast. AE, MC, V. Map p 124.*

★★ **The Garden** *WINE BAR/ITALIAN* You can either order a bottle of wine from the 1,000-strong list and a plate of cheese and *prosciutto* or sit down to a full meal on the top-floor terrace. *Corso Italia 50.* ☎ *081/8781195. Entrees 8–18€. AE, MC, V. Lunch & dinner Tues–Sun. Closed Jan & Feb. Map p 124.*

★★ **La Minervetta** Situated high over the sea just outside town, this stylish hotel offers striking, contemporary interior design and the atmosphere of a chic seaside villa. Bedrooms and terraces have infinite views. *Via Capo 25.* ☎ *081/8774455. www.laminervetta.com. 12 units.*

Doubles 150–400€ w/breakfast. AE, DC, MC, V. Closed 2 wks in Jan. Map p 124.

★ **Sant'Anna Da Emilia** *TRADITIONAL/FISH* The waterside terrace at this simple trattoria is a wonderful spot for a plate of spaghetti with clams. *Via Marina Grande 62, Marina Grande.* ☎ *081/8072720. Entrees 7–13€. No credit cards. Apr–Oct Wed–Mon lunch & dinner, Jul & Aug open daily. Map p 124.*

★★★ **Torre del Saracino** *GOURMET* This award-winning restaurant has a lovely terrace overlooking the sea. Chef Gennaro Esposito's menus are based on the freshest seasonal produce and local culinary traditions; the results are exquisite to both the eye and the palate. *Via Torretta 9, Marina di Equa.* ☎ *081/80285. www.torredelsaracino.com. Entrees 28–30€. AE, DC, MC, V. Lunch & dinner Tues–Sat, lunch Sun. Map p 124.*

Sundown on the terrace at the Bellevue Syrene.

The Amalfi Coast

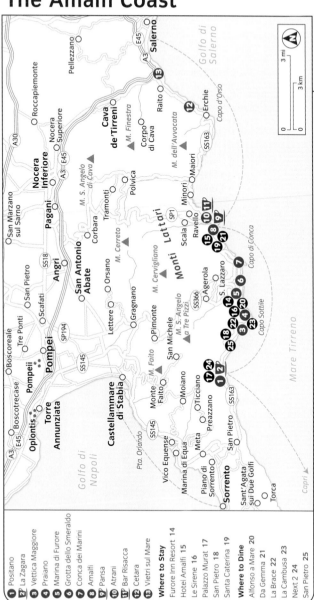

The Amalfi Coast drive clings to rugged cliffsides, and weaves tortuously in and out and up and down gorges from Positano to Amalfi. It is 16km (10 miles) in length, but narrow, and set against a background of shimmering azure sea, olive and lemon groves, purple bougainvillea, and whitewashed villages tumbling down the hillside. You can do the complete tour in a day, but allowing two or three would be much more pleasant. START: **Positano.**

Positano by night.

❶ ★★★ kids Positano. The most famous of the Amalfi Coast towns clings impossibly to an almost sheer cliff-face, its pastel-hued houses tumbled on top of each other, united by narrow pathways and lots of often steep steps. Few people come here to see the 'sights' (there aren't many); they come to stroll the pretty, bougainvillea-draped lanes, to hang out on bar and hotel terraces, and to admire the many unforgettable views.

Positano's History

The town flourished in the 12th and 13th centuries, when its merchant fleet gave rival and neighbor Amalfi a run for its money, but subsequently entered a long decline. So bad was the situation by the mid-1800s that three-quarters of the 8,000 population emigrated to America, leaving the place to regress to a quiet fishing village. Then, after World War II, Positano was 'discovered' by the likes of John Steinbeck, Stravinsky, and Diaghilev and it was only a question of time before the *dolce vita* jet-set moved in; which they did, big time, in the 1960s. Today the town is undeniably picturesque and its natural setting is stunning. However, between late May and September, it's crowded with day-trippers and very expensive. If you want to get a feel for 'old' Positano, come out of season.

Positano

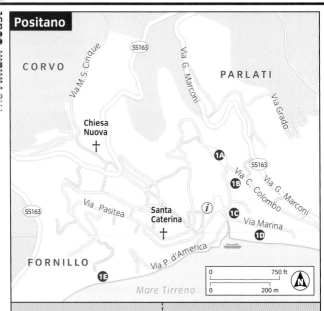

CORVO

Via M. S. Cinque

SS163

Via G. Marconi

PARLATI

Via Grado

Chiesa Nuova ✝

1A

SS163

Via C. Colombo

Via G. Marconi

1B

SS163

Via Pasitea

Santa Caterina ✝

(i)

1C

Via Marina

1D

FORNILLO

Via P. d'America

1E

Mare Tirreno

0		750 ft
0		200 m

N

Park the car, or get off the bus, at the top of the town and walk down to **1A Piazza dei Mulini.** From here, Via dei Mulini descends towards the beach, passing **1B Palazzo Murat** (now a lovely hotel) on the way. This elegant, 18th-century mansion with its gorgeous courtyard garden is one of the few aristocratic period buildings in Positano and once belonged to Gioachino Murat, King of Naples. Farther down the hill lies the church of **1C Santa Maria Assunta** with its typical green and yellow majolica-tiled dome and, inside, a glowing 13th-century *Madonna and Child.* There's always plenty going on at the gray sand and pebble beach of **1D Spiaggia Grande,** a natural meeting place for the locals where restaurants, bars, and pine trees line the curve of sand. Fishing boats are pulled up on the right side of the beach while the left-hand end is occupied by private bathing establishments. The free beach is in the middle. A footpath leads west around the point to **1E Il Fornillo beach,** a good alternative location for a swim.

2 ★ La Zagara. On your way down into town, stop off at this famous pastry shop; it's always crowded with tourists, but that doesn't detract from the delicious pastries and cakes. There's a lovely terrace too. *Via dei Mulini 6.* ☎ *089/ 875964. $.*

3 Vettica Maggiore. Driving east from Positano, after a series of twists and turns around deep gullies, the next towns along the coast are merging Vettica Maggiore and Praiano. There's a small beach in Vettica and a huge piazza above, paved with majolica tiles. There are more bright tiles on the dome and bell tower of the church of **San**

The church of Santa Maria Assunta, Positano.

Gennaro, which houses 16th- and 17th-century altar paintings.

❹ ★★ **Praiano.** Once a center for the silk industry, Praiano makes a good, low-key alternative to Positano for touring the coast. The church of **San Luca** lies at the top of the town and there's a medieval lookout tower on the rocks. Just along the coast is the tiny, picturesque fishing hamlet of **Marina di Praia,** a clutch of cottages, a couple of restaurants (including Alfonso al Mare, see p 139), and a few boats pulled up on a tiny beach squeezed between walls of towering rock.

❺ ★ **Marina di Furore.** From this point, the coastline becomes quite wild. The **Vallone di Furore,** a deep, fjord-like gully opening onto the sea a couple of kilometers east of Praiano, is a case in point. A viaduct crosses the gorge and steps from the top lead down to the miniscule hamlet of Marina di Furore, literally just a scattering of restored pastel-hued huts and fishing boats; it makes a great photo opportunity.

❻ ★★★ **kids** **Grotta dello Smeraldo.** The Emerald Grotto that lies just before **Conca dei Marini** justly attracts the crowds. You can take the elevator from the main road down the sheer cliff to a watery cave, complete with huge stalagmites and stalactites, where you will be loaded into a rowing boat; or you can (and this is the more pleasant option) catch a boat from a neighboring port and arrive by sea. The name comes from the intense blue/green light that filters into the cave from an underwater crevice; it's at its best between about noon and 3pm. ⏱ *1½ hr; go at lunchtime or in the afternoon to avoid crowds. On the main coast road 1km (0.6 mile) west of Conca*

Marina di Furore.

Those Were The Days...

In its heyday, between the 9th and 12th centuries, Amalfi was a glorious maritime republic with 70,000 inhabitants, rival to mighty powers such as Pisa and Genoa. It minted its own money and made its own laws. With its ideal topography (steep hillsides cut by fast streams for powering mills), the town also became an important center for papermaking in the 1200s, when local artisans began producing the prized material that was to replace parchment. Even after the fall of the Republic to Pisa, prosperity continued until a devastating earthquake all but destroyed the town in 1343 and Amalfi slipped into oblivion. Centuries later, along came the same literary and artistic travelers who 'discovered' Capri, Ravello, and other coastal delights, catapulting Amalfi onto the tourist map. Nowadays, the town's former glory is commemorated annually in the Regata Storica, a boat race that rotates between rivals Amalfi, Pisa, Genoa, and Venice.

dei Marini. ☎ *089/871107. Admission 5€. Nov–Mar daily 10am–3pm, Apr–Oct daily 9am–4pm.*

⑦ Conca dei Marini. This town, once an important naval base of the Amalfi Republic, is spread vertically over a hillside. Down on the shore is the picturesque little harbor with the tiny chapel of **Santa Maria della Neve.** In the upper part of the town (accessed via the road to Agerola), a

muddle of white, flat-roofed houses tumbles down the slope, mingling with terraced gardens and panoramic views. There are three churches up here, all with fabulous settings; neo-Byzantine **San Pancrazio,** the convent of **Santa Rosa** (used as a spectacular venue for the Festival of Ravello, p 164), and **Sant'Antonio di Padova.**

Marina Grande, Positano.

8 ★★★ **kids** **Amalfi.** It's difficult to imagine today that Amalfi could ever have been home to 70,000 souls. Although the largest town on this tour, it's a gorgeous little resort of just 5,000 inhabitants with a vaguely sleepy air, its jumble of white buildings clinging to the sides of a deep gully.

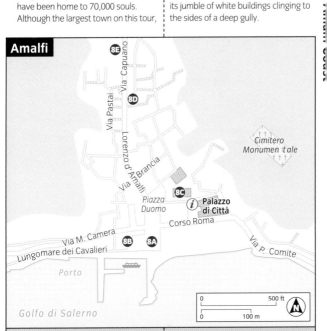

Amalfi

Via Capuano · **8E**
Via Pastai · **8D**
Lorenzo d'Amalfi
Via Brancia
Cimitero Monumentale
8C
Piazza Duomo · *i* **Palazzo di Città**
Corso Roma
Via M. Camera · **8B** · **8A**
Lungomare dei Cavalieri
Via P. Comite
Porto
Golfo di Salerno

0 — 500 ft
0 — 100 m
N

From busy **8A** **Piazza Flavio Gioia,** **8B** **Porta della Marina** leads to Piazza Duomo and the 9th–12th-century Arab–Norman style **8C** **Duomo di Sant'Andrea** (☎ 089/871324), which dominates from the top of its monumental staircase. The grand, striped and arched black-and-white façade is a reconstruction, but the central bronze doors were made in Constantinople in 1066 and are possibly the oldest in Italy. The ancient **Chiostro del Paradiso** has delicate interlaced Moorish arches, evidence of the strong trade links that Amalfi once had with north Africa. At the back is the austere Romanesque **Cappella del Crocifisso,** the original church with 14th-century frescoes. Steps lead down to the marble **crypt** that contains St. Andrew's bones and up again into the blandly restored cathedral itself.

Head up Via Lorenzo d'Amalfi; on either side is a series of atmospheric old alleyways such as the tunnel-like **8D** **Ruga Nova Mercatorum,** medieval Amalfi's main thoroughfare. Via delle Cartiere leads to the **8E** **Museo della Carta** (☎ 089/8304561) and the Valle dei Mulini where Amalfi's famous paper mills were sited. The museum, housed in a 15th-century mill, documents the history of this ancient craft.

Charming Atrani.

Amalfi, but if time permits, there are a few more interesting stops along the coast. About a kilometer east of Amalfi lies charming little Atrani, one-time residential quarter of the larger town. Life here bustles around **Piazza Umberto I.** The 10th-century church of **San Salvatore de' Bireto** with its pretty clock and bell tower once hosted the investitures of Amalfi's doges (rulers) and stands at the top of a flight of stairs on the north side of the square. Like those of Amalfi's Duomo, its bronze doors were cast in the 11th century in Constantinople and inside there's a Byzantine relief in marble showing two peacocks (symbols of immortality). At the time of writing, however, the church was closed for restoration and isn't likely to reopen any time soon.

9 ★★★ **Pansa.** This old-fashioned pastry shop and café turns out exemplary versions of local specialties such as *torta di limone* (lemon cake) and chocolate *torta Caprese*, a kind of local chocolate cake. There's a nice terrace too. *Piazza Duomo 40.* ☎ *089/871065. $.*

10 ★ **Atrani.** For many people, the classic Amalfi Coast drive finishes in

11 **Bar Risacca.** One of several bars on the small square from where you can soak up the simple, local life, Risacca serves anything from coffee and cakes to light meals and evening cocktails. *Piazza Umberto I 16.* ☎ *089/872866. $–$$.*

12 ★★ **kids** **Cetara.** Working east from Atrani, the coast road passes by **Minori** and **Maiori** (which has the longest beach in the area) and some more impressive coastal scenery before reaching the lazy little fishing

Getting Around the Amalfi Coast

Out of season, the best way to do this tour is undoubtedly by car; it allows more scope for improvisation. However, the coast road between Positano and Amalfi is notoriously clogged with head-to-tail coaches and cars in the high season, which rather puts a damper on the enjoyment of it all. Public buses are subject to the same sorts of traffic jams. To avoid this, use the excellent **Metro del Mare** (☎ 199/600700; www.metrodelmare.com), a fast, regular *aliscafi* (hydrofoil) service that runs between late April and mid-November linking Naples with Sorrento, Positano, Amalfi, and Minori.

The beach at Cetara.

village of **Erchie,** situated around a curving bay. Another 3km (1.8 miles) farther on, **Cetara** is a hard-working, attractive seaside town built into a deep valley that was once the eastern frontier of the Amalfi Republic. It's a lively, untouristy place with a still-thriving fishing industry, famous for its salted anchovies and *colatura di alici* (a kind of anchovy sauce that derives from an ancient Roman recipe). The sauce makes a good souvenir to take home and all the *alimentari* (delis) on the main street running off the harbor sell it.

⓭ ★ Vietri sul Mare. The last stop on the tour is this world famous center for the production of colorful majolica ceramics. Pottery has been made in the area since Roman times, but it was in the early Middle Ages that the ceramics industry really blossomed; in the late 11th century, there were 50 kilns in the town. Many of the buildings along this part of the coast are decorated with local majolica work including Vietri's own 18th-century church of **San Giovanni Battista,** which has a tiled dome. There's plenty of opportunity to buy ceramics in Vietri; many of the factories and their retail outlets are in the modern, upper town while the older, more characteristic *centro storico* is down by the sea. The name Solimene dominates: various branches of this family have been making colorful ceramics for generations. *Outlets are in Via G Mazzini 1 (☎ 089/211878), Via 24 Luglio 15 (☎ 089/210048), and outside the center in Località Fontana Vecchia (☎ 089/ 210188).*

Where to **Stay**

★ **kids** **Furore Inn Resort** A small, luxurious, resort-style hotel spread over a sea-facing hillside, this place offers myriad facilities including two restaurants, bars, three pools, a swish spa, and tennis courts. *Via dell'Amore, Contrada S. Elia, Furore.* ☎ *089/8304711. www. furoreinn.it.22 units. Doubles 260–460€ w/breakfast. AE, DC, MC, V. Map p 130.*

★ **Hotel Amalfi** This modest mid-range hotel offers clean, decently furnished rooms (some with a balcony), a pretty garden, and a roof terrace where breakfast is served. The location is excellent and the welcome friendly. Open all year. *Vico dei Pastai 3.* ☎ *089/872440. www.hamalfi.it. 40 units. Doubles 70–150€. AE, MC, V. Map p 130.*

★★ **Le Sirene** This delightful, simple little hotel with genuinely welcoming owners is set on a hillside in terraced gardens facing Positano across the bay from Praiano. There's a rooftop terrace for sunbathing. *Via San Nicola 10, Praiano.* ☎ *089/874013. www.lesirene.com. 12 units. Doubles 90–100€. MC, V. Map p 130.*

★★★ **Palazzo Murat** Housed in an 18th century ex-royal residence, this elegant hotel boasts public areas and bedrooms furnished with antiques and a flower and a gorgeous plant-filled courtyard garden. The excellent restaurant, **Il Palazzo,** serves a creative take on local dishes. *Via dei Mulini 23.* ☎ *089/ 875177. www.palazzomurat.it. 30 units. Doubles 150–475€ w/breakfast. AE, DC, MC, V. Map p 130.*

★★★ **San Pietro** Despite its luxurious facilities and immaculate service, this hotel, built into the side of a sheer cliff, is in no way pompous. An elevator whisks you down to the open reception area, panoramic terrace, and the gorgeous sunny rooms (all with terraces). At the bottom, there's a private beach and restaurant. In all, a real treat. *Via Laurito 2.* ☎ *089/875455. www.ilsanpietro.it. 61 units. Doubles 420–950€ w/breakfast. AE, DC, MC, V. Map p 130.*

★★★ **Santa Caterina** Amalfi's best hotel sits above the coast just west of town. Done out in classy Mediterranean style, the bedrooms all have sea-facing terraces. There are extensive grounds, a spa, a great pool and private beach, and an excellent restaurant. *Via Nazionale 9.* ☎ *089/871012. www.hotel santacaterina.it. 49 units. Doubles 240–710€. AE, DC, MC, V. Map p 130.*

Hotel San Pietro, Positano.

Where to **Dine**

Beachside dining at Alfonso a Mare, Marina di Praia.

★★ **kids** **Alfonso a Mare** *FISH* Try to fit in a meal on the beach at the divine little fishing village of Marina di Praia. Alfonso serves the likes of octopus salad, *paccheri* (giant pasta tubes) with tuna and capers, and grilled swordfish on bright ceramic plates. *Via Marina di Praia, Praiano.* ☎ *089/874161. www.alfonsoamare.it. Entrees 7–18€. MC, V. Lunch & dinner daily Mar–Oct. Map p 130.*

★★ **Da Gemma** *FISH & TRADITIONAL* This elegant, popular Amalfi restaurant serves fantastic *zuppa di pesce* (chunky fish soup) and other fishy classics alongside a few meat options such as *paccheri alla Genovese* (pasta tubes served with an oniony meat sauce). *Via Fra' Gerardo Sasso 10, Amalfi.* ☎ *089/ 871345. www.trattoriadagemma. com. Entrees 20–35€. AE, DC, MC, V. Lunch & dinner Thurs–Tues. Closed mid-Jan–mid-Feb. Map p 130.*

★★ **kids** **La Brace** *TRADITIONAL & PIZZA* With its terrace facing Positano, this is a fine place for fish and meat dishes and excellent pizza. *Via Capriglione 146, Praiano.* ☎ *089/ 874226. Entrees 5–20€. MC, V. Lunch & dinner daily Mar–Oct, Nov–Feb lunch & dinner Thurs–Tues. Map p 130.*

★ **La Cambusa** *FISH & TRADITIONAL* This beachfront restaurant serves reliable fish and seafood staples such as spaghetti with mussels and cherry tomatoes or linguine with lobster. Book a table on the balcony. *Piazza Vespucci 4, Positano.* ☎ *089/ 875432. Entrees 12–45€. AE, DC, MC, V. Lunch & dinner daily Apr–Oct, Nov–Mar Wed–Sun lunch & dinner. Closed 3 wks in Jan. Map p 130.*

★★★ **Next 2** *FISH & TRADITIONAL* Offering an interesting menu based on local dishes and a fine wine list, this stylish, contemporary restaurant and wine bar has a buzzy, young vibe. The regularly changing menu features the likes of *paccheri* stuffed with ricotta and spinach and tuna steak with asparagus. *Via Pasitea 242, Positano.* ☎ *089/8123516. www.next2.it. Entrees 14–19€. AE, MC, V. Dinner daily Easter–Nov. Map p 130.*

★★ **San Pietro** *FISH* Cetara's fish-based local cuisine is given a creative take at this lovely restaurant. Book a table on the terrace and order the generous mixed fish antipasto followed by risotto with tuna roe and smoked *provola*. *Piazzetta San Francesco 2, Cetara.* ☎ *089/261091. Entrees 25–45€. AE, MC, V. Lunch & dinner daily Jun–Sep, Wed–Mon Oct–May. Map p 130.*

Ravello

1 Al San Domingo
2 Duomo
3 Museo del Corallo
4 Villa Rufolo
5 Emporio Ravello
6 San Giovanni del Toro
7 Villa Cimbrone

Where to Stay & Dine

Cumpà Cosimo 8
Hotel Caruso 9
Rosellini's 10
Villa Giordano 11
Villa Maria 12

The coastal road and towns below are often choked with cars and tour buses, but Ravello's traffic-free status gives it an air of classy tranquility and when the day-trippers have left, it reverts to being a sleepy, hilltop village. For such a tiny place, there's actually quite a lot to see; together with the views and atmosphere that more than justify an overnight stay. START: **Piazza Duomo.**

1 ★ **Al San Domingo.** Start the day with a cappuccino in harmonious Piazza Duomo. Of the several bars and cafés in the square, this is the most elegant and has a large alfresco terrace. *Piazza Duomo 2.* ☎ *089/857142. $.*

2 ★★★ **Duomo.** Ravello's cathedral was founded in 1086 and boasts a fine set of medieval bronze doors. Although the interior of the church was 'baroqued' in the 17th

century, the gilt and marble was ripped out in the 1980s and the luminous space was restored to its late medieval form. The two pulpits halfway down the central nave are magnificent; the higher one dates from 1272 and is supported by six twirling, candy-stick columns with mosaic decorations resting on grinning (or snarling?) lions. Mosaics on the other pulpit show Jonah being gobbled up by the whale although the whale looks more like a dragon with wings. The small museum in the crypt contains a collection of

The coastline seen from Ravello.

architectural bits and pieces plus some precious gold and silver work. 🕐 *45 min. Piazza Duomo.* ☎ *089/858311. www.chiesaravello.com. Church: Free admission. Daily 8:30am–1pm, 3–8pm. Museum: 2€. Apr–Oct daily 9:30am–1pm & 3–7pm, Nov–Mar Sat & Sun only.*

❸ ★ Museo del Corallo. This interesting little museum documents the history of local artisans' work in coral, which has long been gathered in the area and used to make exquisite cameos, religious and domestic objects, and jewelry. 🕐 *30 min. Piazza Duomo 9.* ☎ *089/857461. Free admission. Mon–Fri 10am–2pm & 3–5pm.*

❹ ★★ Villa Rufolo. Accessed through the tower facing Piazza del Duomo, Villa Rufolo was built in Norman–Arab style by the super-rich Rufolo family in the 13th century. Fast-forward to 1851 and the near-derelict villa was bought by Francis Reid, a Scotsman who breathed life back into the house and the gorgeous gardens, which became something of a Mecca for artists

and musicians. Today, highlights include the Moorish cloister and the belvedere with its staggering views, a magical setting for the world-class concerts of the **Festival di Ravello** (www.festivaldiravello.com). 🕐 *1 hr. Piazza Duomo 1.* ☎ *089/857621. www.villarufolo.it. Admission 5€ adults, 3€ over-65s and under-12s. Daily 9am–30 min. before sunset; closes 5pm on concert days.*

❺ ★ Emporio Ravello. I suggest a picnic lunch in the shady little public garden the top of Via Wagner. This deli is well stocked with everything for a feast: fresh mozzarella and other cheeses, hams and salami (made by the owner), bread, wines, and beer. *Via Roma 8.* ☎ *089/857256. $.*

❻ ★★ San Giovanni del Toro. A left turn takes you past several of Ravello's upmarket hotels to this 11th-century church with its typically undulating roof. The triple portico is topped with lunettes and the interior has an unusual triple apse, a grand 12th-century mosaic-decorated pulpit, and a

Coral Museum.

crypt with ancient frescoes. ⏱ *30 min. Piazza San Giovanni del Toro. No phone. Free admission. Opening times vary; contact the tourist office (☎ 089/ 857096).*

❼ ★★★ **Villa Cimbrone.** To get an insider take on Ravello's other great villa, you need to book into the luxury hotel that now occupies it, but its glorious grounds are open to all. This grandiose garden, suspended high over the azure sea below, is among the most beautiful in Italy. It was created in 1905 by Lord Grimthorpe, the designer of London's Big Ben. In the 1920s, the villa became a popular hangout for the literary Bloomsbury set, and Greta Garbo hid here in 1937 with her lover, conductor Leopold Stokowsky. Following the map they give you at the ticket office, look out for the Sicilian/Arabic-style cloister, the 'Gothic' crypt, the *tempietto* of Bacchus (a small temple and site of Lord Grimthorpe's tomb), and Eve's Grotto. The central Avenue of Immensity leads to the high point of the garden, the Belvedere of Infinity, which has dizzying views over the Bay of Salerno. ⏱ *1 hr. Via Santa Chiara 26.* ☎ *089/857459. www.villacimbrone.com. Admission 5€ adults, 4€ under-12s. Daily 9am– 30 min. before sunset.*

Ravello: A Bit of History

Although included on any classic Amalfi Coast tour, refined Ravello, perched on a 350m (1,170-ft) hillside, has a very different feel from its seaside neighbors. The town's golden age came in the 1200s when, as second city in the mighty Amalfi Republic, it boasted a population of around 35,000, whose most wealthy citizens built grand churches, cloisters, villas, and gardens. Its quiet charms have been attracting A-list visitors for hundreds of years: King Charles of Anjou, the poet Boccaccio, Richard Wagner, D.H. Lawrence, and Greta Garbo to name just a few.

Where to **Stay & Dine**

Lunch at Villa Maria.

★ **kids** **Cumpà Cosimo** *TRADITIONAL* Nettie Bottone's popular trattoria is often crowded with tourists, but the generous portions of good, home-cooked food justify a visit; Jackie O and Gore Vidal thought so. *Via Roma 46. ☎ 089/857156. Entrees 12–28€. AE, MC, V. Lunch & dinner daily Apr–Oct, Nov–Mar lunch & dinner Tues–Sun. Map p 140.*

★★★ **Hotel Caruso** This luxurious hotel, where 18th-century frescoes and antique furniture rub shoulders with DVD players and flatscreen TVs, has star quality. Views from the glorious gardens (and the heated infinity pool) are extraordinary. *Piazza San Giovanni del Toro 2. ☎ 089/858801. www.hotel caruso.com. 48 units. Doubles 710–920€ w/breakfast. AE, DC, MC, V. Closed Nov–Easter. Map p 140.*

★★ **Rosellini's** *GOURMET* If you feel like a fine dining experience, the panoramic terrace of romantic Rosellini's is the place. Chef Pino Lavarra gives regional, seasonal dishes the creative treatment with fine results. *Hotel Palazzo Sasso, Via San Giovanni del Toro 28. ☎ 089/818181. Entrees 35–55€. AE, DC, MC, V. Lunch & dinner daily. Closed Nov–Mar. Map p 140.*

★★ **kids** **Villa Giordano** Cheaper than its sister, Villa Maria, this hotel has a shady garden with a pool and sunny modern rooms with balconies. Some rooms are big enough for families. *Via Trinità 14. ☎ 089/857170. 33 units. Doubles 160–185€ w/breakfast. AE, DC, MC, V. Closed Nov–Easter. Map p 140.*

★★★ **Villa Maria** This lovely, pink-hued villa is set in a gorgeous garden; views from the terraces and most of the rooms are wonderful. Inside, period furniture and *objets* give the place a homey feel. The restaurant (see below) is one of the best in town. *Via Santa Chiara 2. ☎ 089/857255. www.villamaria.it. 24 units. Doubles 195–240€ w/breakfast. AE, DC, MC, V. Map p 140.*

★★★ **Villa Maria** *CAMPANIAN* The combination of great food and a flower-filled terrace looking out to sea makes a meal here very special. Fresh fish, organic vegetables, and herbs from the garden make up the bulk of the menu; try shrimp and asparagus risotto and sea bass in *acqua pazza* (with tomatoes and herbs). *Via Santa Chiara 2. ☎ 089/857255. www.villamaria.it. Entrees 14–25€. AE, DC, MC, V. Lunch & dinner daily. Map p 140.*

Capri

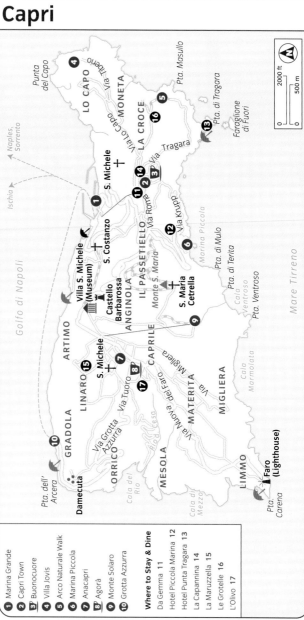

① Marina Grande
② Capri Town
③ Buonocuore
④ Villa Jovis
⑤ Arco Naturale Walk
⑥ Marina Piccola
⑦ Anacapri
⑧ Agorà
⑨ Monte Solaro
⑩ Grotta Azzurra

Where to Stay & Dine

Da Gemma 11
Hotel Piccola Marina 12
Hotel Punta Tragara 13
La Capannina 14
La Maruzzella 15
Le Grotelle 16
L'Olivo 17

The name Capri evokes an unequivocal vision of glamour **and beauty,** a bewitching honeypot for the rich and famous. It was the playground of debauched Roman emperor Tiberius (who spent the last 10 years of his life here and built 12 villas) and continues to draw the international jet-set, despite the day-trippers who invade during the summer months. START: **Marina Grande.**

Back to back designer boutiques, Capri town.

1 Marina Grande. The first impression of Marina Grande, where the hydrofoils dock, is likely to be disappointing, especially if you arrive in high season. Where's the magic? Tourists swarm in their thousands and the area surrounding the port is characterized by cheap souvenir stalls and overpriced restaurants and bars. So get out as quickly as possible; catch the funicular to Capri town. Boats for the Blue Grotto (see **10**) also leave from here. ⏱ *15 min.*

2 ★★★ Capri Town. White-washed Capri town, with its narrow lanes and dazzling white houses, stairways, low arches, and shoulder-to-shoulder designer boutiques, embodies the idea of a chic Mediterranean town. At its center is the world-famous piazzetta.

When To Go

'Capri makes you forget everything,' announced Lenin in 1910 while visiting his friend Maxim Gorky, who had a villa on the island. These days, it's hard to forget it all if you come between late June and early September when day-trippers cram onto the tiny island, testing its resources to the limit. The best way to avoid the (literal) crush is to stay overnight; all but a very small percentage of the tourists leave at the end of the day, as the place heaves a sigh of relief and settles into something resembling a genuine island atmosphere, albeit a very chic island.

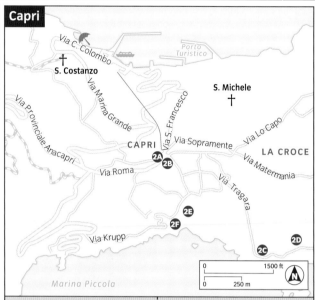

Capri

Via C. Colombo

S. Costanzo

Porto Turistico

Via Marina Grande

S. Michele

Via Provinciale Anacapri

Via S. Francesco

Via Sopramente

Via Lo Capo

CAPRI

LA CROCE

2A

2B

Via Matermania

Via Roma

Via Tragara

2E

2F

2D

2C

Via Krupp

Marina Piccola

0 — 1500 ft
0 — 250 m

Start the tour from the terrace right above the funicular station, with its impressive views down to Marina Grande. From here, walk past the clock tower and into the famously picturesque **2A Piazza Umberto I** (aka *La Piazzetta*), through which every visitor passes at some point. A drink on the terrace of any of the four celebrated cafés is a must for some prime (and pricey) people-watching; the little square is at its best in the evening when the day-trippers have left. The 17th-century **2B Church of Santo Stefano** sits at the top of a flight of steps just above the square and has a characteristic multidomed roof. The classic Capri *passeggiata* or stroll starts in the *piazzetta*, passes the designer boutiques in Via Vittorio Emanuele and Via Camerelle, and finishes at the end of Via Tragara where the **2C Belvedere Tragara** gives you breathtaking views of the three limestone rocks known as the

2D Faraglioni. The farthest is home to bright blue lizards found nowhere else on the planet. The lane down the side of the Quisisana hotel leads to the **2E Certosa di San Giacomo,** a semi-abandoned medieval monastery with a typical cross-barrel roof and simple cloister. Above are the panoramic terraces of the **2F Giardini di Augusto.**

Capri's famous Faraglioni.

3 ★ **Buonocuore.** This place is good for inexpensive coffee and cakes or refreshing ice cream. It also sells delicious pizza, sandwiches, and hot dishes-to-go that make good picnic food. *Via Vittorio Emanuele 35.* ☎ *081/8377826. $.*

4 ★ **Villa Jovis.** From the *piazzetta*, a steep, 40-minute walk beginning in Via Botteghe leads up to Tiberius's vast Villa Jovis, from where the debauched ruler governed his empire between A.D. 27 and 37. Not much is left of the once-luxurious complex, but its position is extraordinary. Apparently, the Emperor threw those who fell from his favor down the 470m (1,550 ft) cliff to the south of the villa known as the **Salto di Tiberio.** ⏱ *2 hrs. (including walk). Viale Amadeo Maiuri.* ☎ *081/8374549. Admission 2€. Daily 9am–1 hr before sunset.*

5 ★★★ **Arco Naturale Walk.** From the Belvedere di Tragara, a circular path involving hundreds of steps and stunning scenery leads round the coast, past the red-painted **Villa Malaparte,** to the cave known as the **Grotta di**

Walking to the Faraglioni, Capri.

Matermania, said to be sacred to the cult of the Goddess Cybele. From the grotto, another path descends to the Arco Naturale, a dramatically towering natural arch formed from eroded rock. ⏱ *1 hr.*

6 ★★ **Marina Piccola.** This charming little resort, located on the south side of Capri and overshadowed by sheer cliffs, is where the chicest private bathing establishments are found. The tortuous footpath that winds back up to the Certosa via a series of tight hairpin bends is known as the **Via Krupp.** ⏱ *1 hr.*

Getting Around and What to See

There are few private cars on Capri (many of the islanders don't even have a driving license) and visitors aren't allowed to bring vehicles to the island. If you're staying over, hotels will usually help transfer your baggage from the port to your hotel. Capri town, Anacapri, Marina Grande, and Marina Piccola are connected by small bus and taxis. Otherwise, you have to walk, and walking here usually involves steps, lots of them. So allow plenty of time for getting from A to B, and wear comfortable shoes. Bearing all this in mind, you really need two whole days to see everything on this itinerary. If you can't stay overnight, concentrate on the following: Capri town mini-tour, Arco Naturale walk, and Anacapri. Throw in the Grotta Azzura if there's time at the end of the day.

7 ★★★ **Anacapri.** The rival towns of Capri and Anacapri led separate existences until 1872, united only by way of the Scala Fenicia (a still-standing flight of nearly 900 steps). Today, Anacapri has a more low-key, rural feel to it and many of the Capresi live here rather than in glitzy Capri itself. In 1874, celebrated Swedish physician Axel Munthe first visited the town and fell for its rural, unworldly charms. He built the impressive **Villa San Michele** (☎ 081/8371401) on the site of one of Tiberius's villas; the grand house and its pristine gardens have become an essential tourist attraction. Via Orlandi leads to the old town center from Piazza Vittoria (where the buses stop), past the red-painted **Casa Rossa** (☎ 081/8382193) built by J.C. MacKowen who wrote the first guidebook to Capri in 1876. Via San Nicola leads to Piazza San Nicola and the church of **San Michele** (☎ 081/8372396), which has a magnificent majolica-tiled floor dating from 1761 illustrating the Garden of Eden complete with Adam and Eve and a host of cute animals. 🕐 *2 hrs.*

8 ★★ **Agorà.** This chic bar/restaurant is a cool place to wind down after a long day with a cocktail and maybe some background jazz. If you're into beer, they make their own and serve tapas-type snacks. *Piazza Caprile 1, Anacapri.* ☎ *081/8372018.* $.

9 ★ **Monte Solaro.** From just off Piazza Vittoria, you can catch a chairlift up over increasingly wild countryside to the dizzy, 600m (2,000 ft) heights of Monte Solaro from where there are eye-popping 360° views. 🕐 *40 min. Chairlift info* ☎ *081/8371428. Ticket 4€ each way, free under-8s. Mar–Oct daily 9:30am–4:30pm, Nov–Feb daily 10:30am–3:30pm.*

10 ★★ **Grotta Azzurra.** Located on the northwest corner of the island, the fabled Blue Grotto is accessible from Marina Grande and from a jetty just below Anacapri by boat (10 minutes walk from Anacapri or take the bus). The magical blue light of Capri's most popular attraction is caused by sunlight reflecting off the white sand floor of the cave. It was 'discovered' by Polish poet August Kopisch in 1826, but the pleasure-seeking Romans, however, had uncovered its delights centuries before when it had been the *nymphaeum* (a sanctuary, often built in a natural grotto, consecrated to water nymphs) of the Roman villa of Gradola. 🕐 *1½ hr. including transport; visit at lunchtime or late afternoon to avoid crowds. Admission 21.50€ from Marina Grande including return transport; 10.50€ from Anacapri. Daily 9am–1 hr. before sunset.*

Grotta Azzurra.

Where to **Stay & Dine**

★ **kids Da Gemma** *PIZZA*   Pizza and a selection of local dishes are served on a large veranda looking down to Marina Grande. *Via Madre Serafina 6, Capri.* ☎ *081/8370461. Entrees 8–20€. AE, MC, V. Aug daily lunch & dinner, Apr–Jul, Sep–Oct Tues–Sun lunch & dinner. Map p 144.*

★★ **Hotel Piccola Marina**   Stylishly modern with views over the bay of Marina Piccola, this newly-refurbished hotel offers a lovely pool, elegant rooms, and reasonable rates. *Via Mulo 14.* ☎ *081/8379642. www.hoteldellapiccolamarina.it. 40 units. Doubles 180–300€ w/breakfast. AE, DC, MC, V. Map p 144.*

★★★ **Hotel Punta Tragara**
This luxury hotel, occupying a villa built by Le Corbusier, boasts what is arguably the best position on the island. Many of the rooms have close-up views of the Faraglioni. There are two pools, glorious terraced gardens, and an excellent restaurant serving traditional cuisine. *Via Tragara 57.* ☎ *081/8370844. www.hoteltragara.com. 44 units. Doubles 370–780€ w/breakfast. AE, DC, MC, V. Map p 144.*

★★★ **La Capannina** *CAMPANIAN*
A good place for celebrity spotting (and, by the way, a great restaurant), La Capannina serves up textbook versions of classics such as cheese-and marjoram and cheese-filled ravioli *alla Caprese* (with tomato sauce). *Via Le Botteghe 12.* ☎ *081/8370732. www.capannina-capri.com. Entrees 14–38€. AE, DC, MC, V. Lunch & dinner daily Mar–Oct. Map p 144.*

★★★ **kids La Maruzzella**
Immersed in the countryside just outside Anacapri, this place offers delightfully rustic rooms, wonderful home-cooked food, and charm in

Punta Tragara's panoramic pool.

buckets. *Via Lo Funno 15, Anacapri.* ☎ *081/8372768. 3 units. Doubles 120€ w/breakfast. No credit cards. Map p 144.*

★★ **Le Grotelle** *TRADITIONAL*
With its panoramic terrace just above the Arco Naturale, this is a place to come on a balmy night with a full moon. The reliable food is almost incidental. *Via Arco Naturale.* ☎ *081/8375719. Entrees 10–26€. MC, V. Lunch & dinner daily July– Aug. Mar–Jun, Sep, Oct Fri–Wed lunch & dinner. Map p 144.*

★★★ **L'Olivo** *GOURMET*   Chef Oliver Glowig offers a creative take on local culinary traditions with spectacular results at this super-stylish, multi-awarded restaurant. *Capri Palace Hotel, Via Capodimonte 2B, Anacapri.* ☎ *081/9780111. www.capri-palace.com. Entrees 28–34€. AE, DC, MC, V. Apr–Oct daily lunch & dinner. Map p 144.*

Ischia

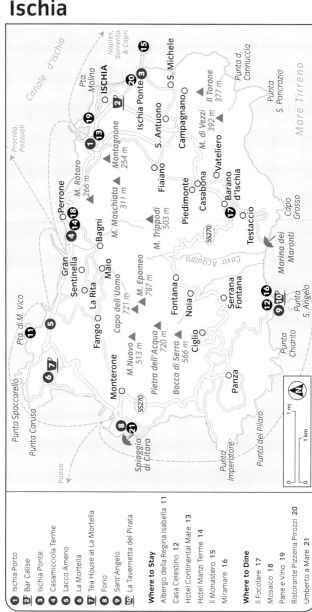

Volcanic Ischia has been famed for its curative waters (the most radioactive in Europe) since ancient Greek times, and tourist activity here still revolves around the 100 plus thermal baths. However, with a population of 60,000 and a ground surface of around 46 sq. km (18 sq. miles), there's more to Ischia than just its spas. You need at least 2 nights to get a feel for the place. START: **Ischia Porto.**

①　Ischia Porto. If you arrive in the main ferryport, you may notice the naturally round harbor, which is, in fact, an extinct volcanic crater. Once a landlocked lake, it was only connected to the sea by King Ferdinando II in 1854. Today, Ischia Porto is a typically attractive Mediterranean port, colorful and bustling with a yacht-filled marina and plenty of restaurants and bars strung out along the water's edge. The King used to bathe in the thermal waters at the **Antiche Terme Comunali** (now government offices) on Via Iasolino, a block in from the port, and in 1854, he built the church of **Santa Maria di Portosalvo** just to the west. Although I wouldn't advise staying in Ischia Porto (it's too crowded), it is a good reference point for the rest of the island; the main tourist office is here, plus a bank and post office and you can catch a bus to other parts of the island. The bus stops are just

beyond Santa Maria di Portosalvo and there's a taxi rank opposite the ferry ticket offices. 🕐 *1 hr.*

②　Bar Calise. Located in a pine tree-filled park roughly between Ischia Porto and Ischia Ponte, this historic bar is a very popular spot for morning cappuccino and cakes or an excellent ice cream. *Piazza degli Eroi 69.* 📷 *081/991270. $.*

③　★★ kids Ischia Ponte. Although once separate towns, Ischia Porto and the slightly classier Ischia Ponte have merged into one these days. The town is dominated by the vast **Castello Aragonese** (📷 081/992834), which sits brooding atop its 100m (330-ft) high rocky islet, joined to the mainland by a solid causeway. Today, the castle is privately owned and contains an atmospheric hotel (see p 156), but is open to visitors; allow 1½ to 2 hours

Fishing boats in Ischia Porto.

Castello Aragonese, Ischia Ponte.

to fully appreciate its magic. An elevator whisks you to the upper level from where two itineraries cover the key features of the citadel, leading through rooms of the ancient buildings and beautifully-kept terraces with fabulous views all around. There's an open-air bar/restaurant at the very top, a perfect spot for a panoramic coffee.

There's not much else to see in Ischia Ponte, but the old streets are lined with bright shops, bars, and cafés. Pop into the **Cattedrale dell'Assunta** on Via Mazzella to see the 14th-century baptismal font and a Romanesque wooden crucifix. There's a good beach here too, the **Spiaggia dei Pescatori,** where fishermen and their colorful little boats share the sand with sunbathers. ⏱ *half a day.*

❹ ★ **Casamicciola Terme.** The presence of Casamicciola's thermal waters were documented as early at the 1st century A.D. when Pliny the Elder described the town's Gurgitello spring. The spa resort was born in the early 19th century (making it the oldest on the island) when luxurious hotels were built to accommodate visitors seeking the medicinal benefits of the waters (said to be particularly effective in the treatment of rheumatic, arthritic, and respiratory problems), and it became a popular stop on the Grand Tour. Disaster struck, however, in 1883 when an earthquake all but destroyed the town killing 2,300 people. Today, Casamicciola has been rebuilt. It was renamed Casamicciola Terme in recognition of the fact that it now thrives on the commercialization of its radioactive thermal waters, which bubble out of the ground at around 160°C (320°F) (the water is cooled before you bathe in it!). Tens of thousands of annual visitors book into its many hotels for a week or so of therapeutic cures. The rather sprawling town doesn't really have a center as such, but **Piazza Marina,** by the ferry port, is a hub. ⏱ *30 min.*

❺ ★★ **Lacco Ameno.** Some of Italy's earliest Greek settlers made their home on the site of this upmarket resort whose most recognizable landmark is a chunk of weathered volcanic rock that juts out from the sea off the promenade. It's known as *il fungo* (the mushroom). At the western end of town lies **Piazza Santa Restituta,** named after Ischia's patron saint who was martyred in the 3rd century. A basilica was built in her honor, to be replaced in 1036 with the present pink-hued church that stands on the square. Excavations have revealed the remains of the early basilica and a Roman necropolis, which you can visit in the dusty old **Area Archeologico di Santa Restituta** (☎ 081/980538). Lacco Ameno is home to Ischia's most important museum, the **Museo Archeologico di Pithecusae** (☎ 081/900356), housed in Villa Arbusto up the hill. The Greek and Roman artifacts on display proudly include 'Nestor's Cup,' a kotyle vase dating from around 740 B.C. that originated in a necropolis on Rhodes. The azure **Baia di San Montano** is among the island's best beaches and a marvelous place for a refreshing swim. ⏱ *2 hrs.*

⑥ ★★★ La Mortella. This famous, exotic garden was designed by landscapist Russell Page in the mid-1950s for the English composer Sir William Walton and his young Argentine wife Susana. The garden, laid out in a valley with steep, terraced sides, features both species from South America and indigenous plants along with fountains and ponds, sculptures, an Orchid house, an aviary, a Thai pavilion, and plenty of benches for quiet contemplation with wonderful views. There's a small museum dedicated to Walton's life and work, a shop and a tea house. Concerts are held here in the summer. ⏱ *1½ hr.*

⑦ ★★ Tea House at La Mortella. Here you can order a pot of real English tea and a piece of cake. The tea house is half way up the garden and has a large, shady terrace. *Via Francesco Calise 39, Forio.* ☎ *081/986220. $.*

⑧ ★★ Forio. Lying on the west coast, Forio is the largest town on the island and offers Ischia's best sunsets. It's a popular resort with excellent sandy beaches only a seagull's spit away, good restaurants, and some interesting sights to visit. Shop-lined, pedestrian **Corso Umberto** runs through the heart of the town. About half way along is **Piazza Matteotti,** a shady

Santuario della Madonna del Soccorso, Forio.

Sant'Angelo.

square with pastel-colored houses and a clutch of cafés. From here, Via Torrione leads to the solid tower known as **Il Torrione** that dates from 1480, one of a dozen watch-towers built by the Saracens to defend Forio from frequent pirate raids. Back on the Corso, the church of **Santa Maria di Loreto** has a decorated wooden ceiling but rather too much elaborate marble-work for my taste. The picturesque, whitewashed church of the **Madonna del Soccorso** stands in a fantastic situation on its own little headland jutting out to sea to the west of the town. Inside, the model ships sitting on the high balustrade are offerings to the Madonna from sailors who have survived ship-wreck. ⏱ *2 hrs.*

9 ★★★ **kids** **Sant'Angelo.** The fishing village-turned-resort of Sant'Angelo is situated on Ischia's southernmost tip. Just offshore lies the **Punta di Sant'Angelo,** joined to the mainland by an isthmus of sand and guarded by a crumbled old watchtower. You can either hire a

Castello Aragonese

This little island was settled and fortified by the Greeks from Syracusa in the 5th century B.C. and subsequently inhabited by the Romans, the Goths, the Saracens, and many others who fixed their coveting eyes on Naples across the bay. For the Ischians, the fortress has been a place of refuge over the centuries from both invasion and volcanic eruption; they fled here in 1301 when Mount Epomeo erupted and built the ex-Cattedrale dell'Assunta in the same year, incorporating an earlier chapel into its crypt where you can still see fragmented frescoes by followers of Giotto. In the mid-15th century, Alfonso of Aragon rebuilt the by-now crumbling castle and added the causeway. By the early 18th century, the huge citadel was home to some 2,000 families, 13 churches, and a convent. The church was badly damaged by the British in 1809 during the Napoleonic wars, but its ruined dome still dominates the skyline.

Where To Wallow

With 103 hot water springs on the island, many of Ischia's hotels have their own thermal pools and onsite spas, some of which are truly luxurious. A fun alternative to these are the 'spa gardens,' non-residential resorts set in extensive tropical gardens with a private beach, which offer a range of facilities. The two best known are the stylish **Negombo** (☏ 081/986152; www.negombo.it), just outside Lacco Ameno, and more traditional **Poseidon** (☏ 9087111; www.giardiniposeidon.it) located near Forio. Both have multiple thermal pools, a private beach, bars, and restaurants, and offer a vast range of spa treatments (at extra cost), which include all kinds of massages, mud treatments, and beauty routines. A slightly less upmarket alternative is the **Aphrodite Apollon** (☏ 081/999219; www.aphrodite.it), situated above the Maronti beach at Sant'Angelo; if you can't face the walk around the footpath from the village, catch a free taxi boat from the port.

boat-taxi or take the clifftop path east to the long and beautiful beach, the **Spiaggia dei Maronti,** where fumaroles off steam hiss out from between the rocks. Apparently, the restaurant situated in the middle offers eggs and chicken cooked in the sand. The hot spring at **Cava Scura** lies up a steep valley; follow the signs from the beach. ⏱ *1 hr.*

🔟 ★★ **La Tavernetta del Pirata.** The laid back Pirate's Tavern overlooks Sant'Angelo's little harbor, and is a great place to wind down at the end of the day with an *aperitivo.* Snacks include delicious *zingare,* the local toasted sandwich made with mozzarella, prosciutto, and tomatoes. *Via Sant'Angelo 77.* ☏ *081/999251. $–$$.*

Bathers enjoying the restorative thermal waters of one of Ischia's many spas.

Where to **Stay**

★★★ **Albergo della Regina Isabella**
Ischia's grandest hotel enjoys an enviable position on the sea and boasts a spa and three restaurants. Recent restyling has left period features, such as the fabulous tiled floors, intact while giving the place a contemporary feel. *Piazza Santa Restituta 1, Lacco Ameno.* ☎ *081/994322. www. reginaisabella.it. 128 units. Doubles 190–760€ w/breakfast. AE, DC, MC, V. Map p 150.*

★ **Casa Celestino**
This bright, contemporary Mediterranean-style small hotel sits on the road leading down into Sant'Angelo. The stylish, sunny rooms all have sea-facing terraces. Meals are served overlooking the sea. *Via Chiaia di Rose 20, Sant'Angelo.* ☎ *081/999213. www. hotelcelestino.it. 20 units. Doubles 175–250€ w/breakfast. AE, MC, V. Map p 150.*

★ kids **Hotel Continental Mare**
The lush terraced gardens overlooking the sea and the two pools (one particularly suitable for youngsters) make this hotel, located a short hop from Ischia Porto, a good family option. The bright, modern rooms include suites that sleep four. *Via B Cossa 25, Iscia.* ☎ *081/982577. www.continentalmare.it. 57 units. Doubles 130–240€ w/breakfast. AE, DC, MC, V. Map p 150.*

★★★ **Hotel Manzi Terme**
The public spaces at this smart, luxurious hotel in the heart of Casamicciola have a nouveau Pompeiian look while the bedrooms are more classic. There's a stylish, Oriental-style spa, two pools (including a large indoor thermal pool), an award-winning restaurant (Mosaico, see p 157), and exceptionally helpful staff. *Piazza Bagni 4, Casamicciola*

Terme. ☎ *081/994722. www.manzi terme.it. 61 units. Doubles 250–460€ w/breakfast. AE, DC, MC, V. Closed Nov–Easter except 26 Dec–7 Jan. Map p 150.*

★★ **Il Monastero**
The spectacular position of this hotel, at the top of the Castello Aragonese, makes up for the lack of a pool. Bedrooms are stylishly spartan with panoramic views, the restaurant serves delicious organic food, and there's a small spa. *Castello Aragonese 3.* ☎ *081/992435. www.albergoilmonastero.it. 22 units. Doubles 100–160€ w/breakfast. AE, DC, MC, V. Map p 150.*

★★ **Miramare**
This elegant hotel sits on the cliff above Sant'Angelo overlooking Maronti beach. The pretty, modernized bedrooms have lovely views as do the wraparound bar and restaurant terraces. There's a saltwater pool on the roof. *Via Maddalena 29, Sant'Angelo.* ☎ *081/ 999219. www.hotelmiramare.it. 50 units. Doubles 260–450€ w/breakfast. AE, DC, MC, V. Map p 150.*

Thermal pool at the hotel Manzi Terme, Casamicciola.

Where to **Dine**

★★ **kids** **Il Focolare** *TRADITIONAL ISCHITAN* If you're fed up with fish, head to the hills above Casamicciola to this rustic place that serves the best *coniglio all'Ischitana* (rabbit stewed with tomatoes) on the island. There's also artichoke lasagne and chargrilled steak. *Via Cretajo al Crocifisso 3.* ☎ *081/902944. www.trattoriailfocolare.it. Entrees 8–14€. AE, MC, V. Lunch & dinner Fri–Sun, dinner Mon, Tues, & Thurs. Map p 150.*

★★★ **Mosaico** *GOURMET* Dinner at this elegant, upscale restaurant is an extraordinary experience, especially if you book the chef's table in the kitchen. Chef Nino di Costanzo transforms local tastes and culinary traditions into something truly spectacular, a visual as well as a gastronomic feast. *Hotel Manzi Terme, Piazza Bagni 4, Casamicciola Terme.* ☎ *081/994722. www.manziterme.it. Entrees 25–32€. AE, DC, MC, V. Dinner daily. Closed Nov–Easter except 26 Dec–7 Jan. Map p 150.*

★ **Pane e Vino** *TRADITIONAL & PIZZA* Of the many restaurants strung out along Ischia's main port, this place, with its little waterside terrace, stands out. The fish choices (such as linguine with scampi and *fritto misto* (deep-fried seafood)) are tasty, as is the pizza; there are some meat choices too and a good wine list. *Via Porto 24, Ischia Porto.* ☎ *081/991046. Entrees 7–18€. MC, V. Lunch & dinner daily, closed Tues Nov–Mar. Map p 150.*

★ **kids** **Ristorante Pizzeria Pirozzi** *FISH/PIZZA* Although this place serves good fish and seafood, I recommend the tasty pizzas. Start

Fabulous fish at Umberto a Mare.

off with a plate of mixed fried appetizers such as the potato, cheese, and ham-stuffed *crochette* (deep-fried croquettes). *Via Seminario 51, Ischia Ponte.* ☎ *081/983217. Entrees 4–15€. AE, DC, MC, V. Lunch & dinner daily. Map p 150.*

★★★ **Umberto a Mare** *FISH* For a fabulous dinner to the backdrop of an Ischian sunset, book a table on the terrace at Umberto's. The mainly fish-based menu varies with the daily catch; try spaghetti with mullet roe and deep-fried giant prawns with tangy lemon and mint salad. Great wines too. *Via Soccorso 2, Forio.* ☎ *081/997171. www. umbertoamare.it. Entrees 20–27€. AE, MC, V. Lunch & dinner Thurs– Mon, dinner Wed. Map p 150.*

Procida

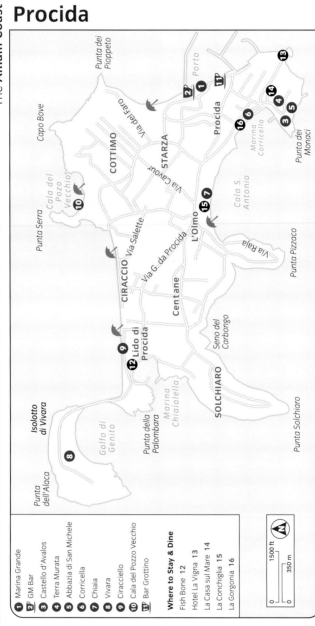

1 Marina Grande
2 GM Bar
3 Castello d'Avalos
4 Terra Murata
5 Abbazia di San Michele
6 Corricella
7 Chiaia
8 Vivara
9 Ciracciello
10 Cala del Pozzo Vecchio
17 Bar Grottino

Where to Stay & Dine

Fish Bone **12**
Hotel La Vigna **13**
La Casa sul Mare **14**
La Conchiglia **15**
La Gorgonia **16**

With 11,000 inhabitants and a surface area of only 3.75 sq. km (1.45 sq. miles), Procida is the most densely populated island in the Mediterranean. Even so, it's a gentle, low-key sort of place (except during July and August) with its own subtle charms, and makes a refreshing change from the glitz and glamour of neighboring Capri and Ischia. START: **Marina Grande.**

① Marina Grande. The car ferries and *aliscafi* that ply the short run from Naples are often full, but most of the passengers will be heading for nearby Ischia's celebrated thermal attractions. Out of season, few tourists disembark on the quayside of pretty Marina Grande, where pastel-colored buildings are strung out along the harbor and fishermen sit in the sun mending their nets. This is the island's main hub and is the place to go for tourist information, ferry tickets, scooter and bike hire, and a selection of reasonably priced restaurants and *pizzerie*. From Marina Grande you can catch a micro-taxi or a bus (or hire a scooter) to other parts of the island. ⏱ *1 hr.*

Marina Grande.

② ★ **GM Bar.** This friendly bar is right opposite the spot where the ferries land, and so it's a good place for a coffee and sweet brioche after the short trip. *Via Roma 117.* ☎ *081/8967560.* $.

③ Castello d'Avalos. The approach to the island from Naples is dominated by the formidable 16th-century Castello d'Avalos, precariously perched over a sheer cliff that plunges down to the sea. Now abandoned, it was used as a prison until 1986. The steep climb up here from the eastern end of Marina Grande to Piazza dei Martiri is

Getting Around

The best way to get around the island is by scooter; be brave and hire one from General Rentals, Marina Grande (☎ 081/8101132). Procida's traffic system is based on a principal 1-way road with a network of smaller, painfully narrow lanes serving the more remote locations. Many of these are lined with high walls, and so it's difficult to get an overall impression of the place from the road. Across the island, tantalizing glimpses are to be had through wrought iron gates of exotic gardens, lemon groves, and small vineyards.

A Bit of History

Procida was first settled by the Mycenaeans between the 15th and 16th centuries b.c. In the Middle Ages, it fell victim to a series of violent Saracen raids that forced the entire population to retreat to the fortified village of Terra Murata at the highest point on the island. The island flourished in the 16th century; you can still see the gracious villas built as holiday homes by visitors from the mainland and the elegant palazzi constructed by prospering shipbuilders. The Bourbon rulers took a shine to Procida and after they acquired the Castello d'Avalos in 1744, they turned the island into a Royal hunting reserve. More recent history has brought strong associations with the sea: flourishing shipyards and an important Naval training school in the 19th century, and a fishing industry that still exists today.

rewarded by views of the painted fishing village of Corricella below, and the castle and Terra Murata above. ⏲ *30 min.*

4 ★★ **Terra Murata.** From Piazza dei Martiri, follow the road up past the castle and then pass through 16th-century **Porta di Mezz'omo** into the walled Terra Murata. In the Middle Ages, frequent attacks by the Saracens forced the islanders to retreat to this, the highest point on the island where they built houses and a church. A handful of families still live in this atmospheric place where the wind whistles through the semi-abandoned buildings. It offers the best views on the island. ⏲ *30 min.*

5 ★★ **Abbazia di San Michele.** Part of a convent complex at the very top of the Terra Murata, this abbey is balanced on the edge of sheer rock and has a beautiful coffered ceiling that includes a painting of the *Archangel Michael* by Luca Giordano (1634–1705). You can also visit the library with its 8,000 or so religious manuscripts, a series of catacombs, and a small museum. ⏲ *1 hr. Terra Murata.* ☎ *081/8969640. www.abbaziasan michele.it. Free admission. Mon–Sat*

9:45am–12:45pm, 3–6pm, Sun 9:45am–12:45pm.

6 ★★★ **Corricella.** From Piazza dei Martiri, steps lead down to the charming fishing village of Corricella with its clutter of pasted-hued houses tumbling down the hillside. If it looks familiar, it may be because the place was used as a location for scenes in the films *Il Postino* and *The Talented Mr. Ripley*. The sheltered quayside is inaccessible to traffic and you can enjoy locally caught fish to a background of lapping water in several waterfront restaurants. ⏲ *1 hr.*

7 ★★ **kids Chiaia.** From Corricella, you can just see the long, gently curving bay of Chiaia to the east, accessible only by sea or by a climb down 180 steps from Piazza Olmo (at the western end of Via Vittorio Emanuele). It's a great place for a swim. ⏲ *2 hr.*

8 ★ **Vivara.** Lying off the northwest tip of Procida is this tiny half-moon islet, actually the tip of a volcanic cone. Traces of Neolithic remains prove that Vivara was inhabited even earlier than Procida. With its unique, unspoilt vegetation, the islet is home to over 150 species of birds plus a

type of rat that walks on it back legs. Vivara (now a nature reserve) is joined to the mainland by a bridge, but at the time of going to press, it was closed for repairs. It should be reopening in the not too distant future; ask at the tourist office for details. 🕐 *1 hr. Free admission.*

9 ★ **kids Ciracciello.** The island's longest and most popular beach stretches out to the east of Vivara. With its dark, volcanic sand, Ciracciello offers both stretches of *spaggia libera* (free beach) and several *stabilimenti balneari* where you can hire sunbeds and umbrellas. The bars and restaurants strung out along the sand make a great spot for a sundowner or an early evening pizza. 🕐 *2 hr.*

10 Cala del Pozzo Vecchio. On the uncrowded eastern part of the island, jutting Punta Serra separates Ciracciello from Cala del Pozzo Vecchio, a delightful small beach with crystal-clear water, which is also known as the beach from *Il Postino* for obvious reasons. Locals scramble over the rocks to the right to reach a series of pretty coves,

Picturesque Corricella.

which make magical bathing spots. In summer, there's a bar here with a talkative gray parrot; a great spot for a cold beer. 🕐 *1 hr.*

11 Bar Grottino. Before you head back on the ferry, call in here, one of the island's best gelaterie, for delicious homemade ice cream and fabulously refreshing lemon granità. *Via Roma 121, Marina Grande.* ☎ *081/8967787. $.*

Cala del Pozzo Vecchio.

Where to **Stay & Dine**

★ **kids** Fish Bone *FISH & PIZZA*
A lively, contemporary restaurant and bar located opposite the yacht moorings in Marina Chiaolella (at the western end of Ciracciello beach), Fish Bone serves great pizza and seafood dishes and hosts live jazz events. *Marina Chiaolella 33.* ☎ *081/8967422. Entrees 3–18€. AE, MC, V. Lunch & dinner Tues–Sun. Map p 158.*

★★ **Hotel La Vigna**   Located within walking distance of Marina Grande, this hotel has simple yet stylish rooms and a small spa. Breakfast is served in a shaded garden, and the hotel's own vineyard produces a crisp white wine. *Via Principessa Margherita 46.* ☎ *081/960469. www.albergolavigna.it. 13 rooms. Doubles 90–200€ w/breakfast. AE, MC, V. Map p 158.*

★ **La Casa sul Mare**   Each of the simply furnished, pretty rooms in this hotel has a little terrace looking over picturesque Coricella. In summer, there's a shuttle boat service to Chiaia beach. *Via Salita Castello 13.* ☎ *081/8968799. www.lacasasulmare.it. 10 units. Doubles 99–168€ w/breakfast. AE, MC, V. Map p 158.*

★★★ **La Conchiglia** *FISH*   This romantic restaurant stands right on Chiaia beach; access is via lots of steps but if you can't face the climb down (and up again), a boat will pick you up in Corricella. Menus are based around the day's catch; pasta with baby clams or mussels and grilled fish. *Spiaggia di Chiaia, access from Via Pizzico 10.* ☎ *081/8967602. Entrees 8–25€. MC, V. Lunch & dinner daily Mar–Oct daily. Map p 158.*

★★ **La Gorgonia** *FISH*   Housed in a pink-washed building on the quayside in Coricella, La Gorgonia serves delicious typical island food: bruschetta with baby octopus, spaghetti with sea urchins (a prized specialty), and a superb *fritto misto*. *Via Marina di Corricella 50.* ☎ *081/8101060. Entrees 10–20€. MC, V. Apr–Oct Tues–Sun lunch & dinner. Map p 158.* ●

What to Eat in Procida

For such a tiny island, Procida's cuisine is surprisingly varied. Typical dishes are based on the abundant seasonal produce to be found on the island and in its surrounding waters: fish and seafood (sea urchins are a specialty; try them on spaghetti), rabbit, vegetables (tomatoes, baby peas, artichokes), wild herbs and giant lemons from which the Procedani make a tart, mint-spiked *insalata di limoni* (lemon salad), lemon cake, *limoncello* (lemon liquer), and a deliciously refreshing *granita al limone* (a kind of lemon sorbet that you drink). Wash it all down with a jug of chilled Luvante, the local white wine.

Before You Go

Government Tourist Offices

In the US 630 Fifth Ave., Suite 1565, New York, NY 10111 ☎ 212/245-5618; 500 N. Michigan Ave., Suite 2240, Chicago, IL 60611 ☎ 312/644-0996; and 12400 Wilshire Blvd., Suite 550, Los Angeles, CA 90025 ☎ 310/820-1898.
In Canada 175 Bloor St E., South Tower, Suite 907, Toronto, ONT M4W 3R8 ☎ 416/9254882.
In the UK & Ireland 1 Princes St., London W1B 2AY ☎ 0207/408-1254.
In Australia Level 4, 46 Market St., Sydney, NSW 2000 ☎ 02/9262-1666.
The official website for the Italian state tourist board is www.italiantourism.com (US & Canada), www.italiantouristboard.co.uk (UK & Ireland), or www.italiantourism.com.au (Australia).

The Best Times to Go

April to June and late September to October are the best months to visit the Naples area. The midsummer months get very crowded, especially in the seaside resorts, despite it becoming uncomfortably hot. Naples itself is an exception; the locals flee the city in August, but it can be unbearably hot. From late October until just before Easter, many shops, restaurants and hotels on the Amalfi Coast and the islands close down completely, but this has its own charms. Winter in Naples on the coast is usually mild with many brilliantly sunny days allowing for alfresco lazy lunches; inland and hilly areas are cooler and wetter.

Festivals and Special Events

SPRING **Easter** (*Pasqua*) is an important religious festival all over Italy. Holy Week sees a program of

Previous page: Spoilt for choice when eating out

special concerts and events in Naples and processions are held on **Good Friday** (*Venerdì Santo*) all over the area; those in Sorrento and the island of Procida are particularly famous.

The **Settimana dei Beni Culturali** is a countrywide event held for one week, usually in April, when all the state-owned museums and galleries are free. The **Maggio dei Monumenti** (☎ 081/5523328, 081/402394) takes place in May; normally impenetrable churches, palazzi, gardens, cloisters, and courtyards in Naples open their doors to the public.

On the first Sunday in May, the first of three annual celebrations of the **feast of San Gennaro**, Naples' revered patron saint, is held. The saint's blood is said to liquefy during a ceremony held in the Duomo.

SUMMER Every 4 years, in June in Amalfi, the splendid **Regata Storica delle Antiche Repubbliche Marinare** is held between the 4 former maritime republics: Amalfi, Genoa, Pisa, and Venice. The next one will be in June 2012. **Concerti al Tramonto** is a series of concerts held June–August in the Villa San Michele, Anacapri (☎ 081/8371401; www.sanmichele.org).

The long summer season in Naples is marked by **Estate a Napoli**, a program of outdoor concerts and other performances all over the city. Still in Naples, 16 July is the feast of **Santa Maria del Carmine** when the bell tower of the eponymous church is 'burnt' with fireworks.

Sorrento holds the **Estate Musicale Sorrentina** (☎ 081/8074033; www.estatemusicalesorrentina.it.) music festival in July and August while the **Festival Musicale di**

NAPLES' AVERAGE DAILY TEMPERATURES & MONTHLY RAINFALL

	JAN	FEB	MAR	APR	MAY	JUNE
Temp. (°F)	50	54	58	63	70	78
Temp. (°C)	9	12	14	17	21	26
Rainfall (in.)	4.7	4	3	3.8	2.4	.8

	JULY	AUG	SEPT	OCT	NOV	DEC
Temp. (°F)	83	85	75	66	60	52
Temp. (°C)	28	29	24	19	16	11
Rainfall (in.)	0.8	2.6	3.5	5.8	5.1	3.7

Ravello (☎ 089/858360; www. ravellofestival.com) hosts concerts featuring internationally-known names in the spectacular setting of the Villa Rufolo gardens. In late July/ early August **Minori's Jazz on the Coast** season features jazz singers and musicians from around the world. Contact the local tourist office (☎/fax 089/877087; www. proloco.minori.sa.it).

On 15 August, the **Feast of the Assumption,** Pozzuoli holds a competition to climb a greased pole and Positano stages a procession and Mass on the beach to commemorate the defeat of the Saracens.

FALL The **Madonna di Piedigrotta** festival is held in the Naples suburb on 7–8 September with processions, music, and fireworks. **San Gennaro's** feast day is celebrated on 19 September in Naples Duomo from 9am.

WINTER The **Feast of the Immacolata** (8 December) sees the beginning of the Christmas celebrations with many families putting up their cribs. From now until Christmas, the streets around San Gregorio Armeno in Naples are packed with people buying nativity figures. Churches all over the region mount their own cribs (*presepi*). During the **Christmas** period, Naples puts on a series of concerts and special

events. **New Year's Eve** (*Capodanno*) is celebrated in Naples with a mega outdoor music bash in Piazza del Plebiscito and fireworks from the Castel dell'Ovo.

The Weather

July and August are very hot in Campania, especially in low-lying areas. The high temperatures begin in Naples in May, often lasting until October. It can also get very humid in Naples in high summer. Winters are mild by the sea, with temperatures averaging 10°C (50°F), but it gets much colder inland and in the mountains, which often are subject to rain and snow.

Useful Websites
www.italiantourism.com: Official site of the Italian government tourist board.
www.trenitalia.it: Italian state railways site.
www.culturacampania.rai.it: Useful site covering museums and attractions throughout Campania.
www.comune.napoli.it: Naples' city council's website (also in English) with practical information, useful contact numbers, and details on the city's museums, monuments, and cultural events.
www.eptnapoli.info: Naples province's excellent site offering information on all aspects of your visit

from museums to hotels and restaurants.

www.napoli.com: Listings site for the city of Naples with events and happenings.

www.campaniartecard.it: Covers museum entrance tickets and transport.

www.campaniatrasporti.it: All public transport (including boats) in Campania.

Cellphones (Mobiles)

If your cellphone is on a GSM system, and you have a multiband phone, you can make and receive calls in the Naples area, but charges can be very high. Assuming that you already have a phone (if not, you can buy one new for around 50€), the best option is to buy a SIM card when you get to Campania. The major Italian networks are Vodafone, Wind, TIM, and 3. A local rechargeable SIM costs about 5€ and gives you far cheaper local calls (under 0.10€/min.). You will need to show photographic ID when buying.

Getting **There**

By Plane

Campania is served by Naples' Capodichino airport (☎ 081/7896259; www.gesac.it). Only Eurofly (☎ 091/5007704; www.eurofly.it) offers transatlantic nonstop flights to Naples from New York. From elsewhere in North America and from Australia and New Zealand, you have to fly first into Rome or Milan and take a short connecting flight. You can also fly nonstop into Naples from most major European airports and from all Italian ones. Alitalia (www.alitalia.com) flies regularly from Rome and Milan into Naples.

If you land in Rome, I recommend catching the train: from Rome's Leonardo da Vinci airport at Fiumicino, an express rail service runs to Roma Termini station which takes 30 minutes and leaves every half-hour. Tickets cost 9.50€ one-way. From Termini, catch one of the frequent, fast Eurostar or Alta Velocità trains to Naples; journey time is about 90 minutes. For timetables, check www.trenitalia.it. From Rome Ciampino airport, catch the Terravision coach (www.terravision.it) to Termini station; journey time is 40 minutes.

Other major airlines flying into Naples include British Airways (www.ba.com), Easyjet (www.easyjet.com), Air France (www.airfrance.com), and Lufthansa (www.lufthansa.com).

Transport from and to the Airport

About 7km (4 miles) northeast of the city center, Capodichino airport is only 15 minutes away from the main train station and 20 minutes from the ferry and hydrofoil docks. The easiest way to get into town is by taking a taxi directly to your hotel: the flat rate for Naples is 12.50€. If you don't have much luggage, the Alibus shuttle bus (☎ 800/639525; www.anm.it) is a cheaper option. Buses leave every 20 minutes from outside the arrivals terminal and stop at the Stazione Centrale in Piazza Garibaldi. Tickets cost 3€. Higher-end hotels on the Amalfi Coast can arrange transfers direct from and to the airport without having to pass through Naples.

By Car

If you arrive in Naples by car, I recommend getting to your hotel as quickly as possible, leaving your bags and parking (the hotel will help you with this, but you will probably have to pay). Don't touch your car again until you want to leave; for reasons NOT to drive in the city, see 'Getting Around,' below. Naples lies on a highly complicated system of highways, but is connected to Caserta, Rome, and Florence to the north by the A1 autostrada, to Salerno, Cosenza, and Reggio Calabria in the south by the A3 autostrada, and with Bari on the southeast coast by the A16 autostrada. Note that all autostrade (highways, signed in blue) are subject to tolls. There's a toll calculator at www.autostrade.it.

By Train

Most trains from other major destinations arriving in Naples pull into Napoli Centrale, the city's principal station in Piazza Garibaldi. From here, you can catch a connection to Sorrento or, via the Circumvesuviana line, to Herculaneum, Pompeii, and Sorrento. If you're staying in Naples, you can catch a taxi to your hotel or, if you haven't much luggage, use the Metro or a bus (see 'Getting Around,' below).

By Boat

Naples is the main port of central Italy, receiving daily ships and ferries from international destinations. A number of cruise-ship companies sail to Naples, especially from spring well into fall. The city is also linked to other Italian ports such as Cagliari, Palermo, and the Aeolian Islands. Arriving in Naples by ship is a magnificent experience and the best approach to Campania. You'll land at the Stazione Marittima, only steps from the Maschio Angioino in the heart of the historic district. From here, you can walk or catch a taxi to your destination. Ferries and hydrofoils also provide invaluable public transport between Naples, the Amalfi Coast, and the islands. See 'Getting Around' for details.

Getting **Around**

By Car

It's total madness to consider hiring a car for use in Naples. The local driving methods are anarchic, traffic is a nightmare, and parking more so. So don't even think about it. A car, however, is a valid way of touring the region, but be warned that in high season (May–September) the coastal roads on the Sorrentine peninsula and Amalfi Coast are choked with nose-to-tail traffic. Ischia (and to a lesser extent Procida) has similar traffic problems and you aren't allowed to take a car onto Capri. So weigh up the pros and cons carefully in advance. Note that all highways (autostrade) in Italy are toll roads, and fuel prices are quite high.

Car Rental

To rent a car in Italy, a driver must have a valid driver's license obtained at least a year before the trip and a valid passport. The minimum age for renting an economy car is 21 and 25 for larger models. Most rental companies will not rent a car to drivers older than 75. Insurance for theft and collision damage is compulsory and can be purchased at any reputable rental firm. You will also need a valid credit card. Besides the major international rental companies—Avis (www.avis.com), Budget (www.budget.com), and Hertz (www.hertz.com)—other companies specializing in European car rentals are Auto

Europe (www.autoeurope.com) and Europe by Car (www.europebycar.com).

By Taxi

Taxis in Naples are safe and relatively cheap. However, beware unofficial cabs that operate in the city; they invariably overcharge unwary tourists. Authorized white taxis can be picked up at signposted ranks (rather than flagged down on the street) or ordered by phone (☎ 081/5525252, 081/5515151, 081/5606666). Your hotel or restaurant will always be happy to phone for a cab when needed. Check that the meter is on at the start of your journey.

By Metro

Metronapoli (☎ 800/568866; www.metro.napoli.it) operates the complex system of under- and overground trains that serve Naples, undoubtedly the fastest way of getting around the city. Metro stations are marked by a large red M; tickets are on sale at tabacchi (tobacconists) and stations and cost 1.10€; they are valid for 90 minutes and can also be used on buses and funicular railways, so you can take several journeys within that time. You must stamp your ticket as you pass through the turnstiles. Work is still in progress on a new, state-of-the-art Metro system linking the suburbs with the city center.

By Funicular Rail

There are four funicular railways in Naples that transport you effortlessly up and down various hills. They are wonderfully old-fashioned but do the job. They are called Centrale, Chiaia, Mergellina, and Montesanto. They operate the same ticket system as the buses and metros (see above); buy tickets in the machines at the stations.

Transport Tip

One ticket covers all. A single ticket costing 1.10€ buys you 90 minutes of journeys on the metro, bus, and funicular railway. So, if you need to catch a metro and the funicular to reach your destination, you can use the same ticket as long as the total journey takes no longer than 90 minutes. Stamp your ticket at the beginning of the first journey.

By Bus

Naples' bus system is operated by ANM (☎ 800/639525, 081/7631111; www.anm.it) and is comprehensive but complicated; the bus map looks like a plate of multicolored spaghetti. Buses are often desperately slow and usually crowded, but you may have to use them to reach areas of the city not covered by the much faster Metro. The only way to reach the Museo di Capodimonte, for example, is by bus; the same applies to Posillipo and Mergellina. Crowded buses are a gift to pickpockets; keep a tight hand on your belongings. Buy your ticket before you board from tabacchi or newsstands; board the bus through the back door and stamp your ticket in one of the machines.

By Train

The train is an excellent way to cover any distance in Campania and the Italian Ferrovia dello Stato (FS for short) train network is very efficient and comparatively cheap. The high speed Eurostar and Alta Velocità trains cost more than Intercity, regionali, or locali trains; contrary to popular belief, they also run on time (mostly). You must reserve a seat on board before you travel; you can do this up to 15 minutes before departure via the website or at a ticket booth in the station. For fares and timetables, consult Trenitalia (☎ 892021 from anywhere in Italy; www.trenitalia.it).

More local to Naples, Sorrento and the Vesuvian attractions of Herculaneum and Pompeii are accessible on the Circumvesuviana line (www.vesuviana.it), which has its own terminal in Corso Garibaldi but is also accessible through the Stazione Centrale. Trains to Pozzuoli and the Campi Flegrei are operated by Ferrovia Cumana (☎ 800/001616; www.sepsa.it) and run from Piazza Montesanto.

By Boat

Car-carrying ferries (traghetti) and faster hydrofoils (aliscafi) are essential modes of transport in this seabound area of Campania. A complex network of routes, operated by some half-dozen different companies, links the islands of Ischia, Procida and Capri, the Sorrentine Peninsula, and the seaside towns on the Amalfi Coast, with Naples. Journey times are short, which means that you can easily take day trips. During the summer months when the roads are often choked with traffic, a boat is often the quickest and certainly the most pleasant way to travel.

Timetables vary during the year with most crossings scheduled in high season; some routes (between Ischia and Capri, for example) only operate between May and September. Timetables (orari) are published each morning in the Il Mattino newspaper, or consult www.campania-trasporti.it. Hydrofoils depart from the Molo Beverello dock in front of the Castel Nuovo in Naples, while ferries leave from the Calata Porta di Massa just to the north. You can buy tickets on the spot; a single hydrofoil ticket from Naples to Ischia or Capri costs 16€. Note that not all ticket offices in smaller ports accept credit cards. Ferries are cheaper than hydrofoils and less affected by bad weather.

Fast **Facts**

APARTMENT RENTALS   If you're planning a longer stay in the Naples area, renting an apartment works out cheaper. **Rent a Bed** (Vico San Carlo alle Mortelle 14, ☎ 081/417721; www.rentabed.com) lists apartments throughout the area covered in this guide. They also list B&Bs.

AREA CODES   081 for the province of Naples (including Sorrento, Pozzuoli, Ischia, and Capri); 089 for the province of Salerno (including the Amalfi Coast). Even calls within the same area code must include the area code.

ATMS   The easiest method of getting instant cash away from home is from an ATM, in Italy called a *Bancomat*. Look out for the Cirrus and PLUS networks which span the globe. ATMs are widespread in Naples and even in smaller towns in the area. Watch out for charges levied by your home bank.

BUSINESS HOURS   Banks are generally open Monday through Friday 8:30am to 1:30pm and 2:30 to 4pm. Shops are usually open Monday through Saturday from 8 or 9am to 1pm and 4:30 or 5pm to 7:30 or 8pm, with one extra half-day closing per week; the day varies from place to place. A growing number of shops in tourist areas stay open during the lunch break and on Sundays.

CAR HIRE   See 'Car Rental' in Getting Around (p 167).

DOCTORS See 'Emergencies.'

DRUGSTORES *Farmacie* (drugstores or pharmacies) often have a green neon cross above their doors. They keep normal shops hours (see 'Business Hours,' above), but in larger towns, Sunday and all-night openings operate on a rotation system. Out of hours, the address of the nearest open pharmacy will be displayed on a poster outside. Language tip: Most minor ailments start with the phrase *mal di*, so you can just say 'Mahl dee' and point to the sore bit (throat, head, stomach, etc.) *Erboristerie*, or herbalist shops, selling traditional herbal remedies are quite common.

ELECTRICITY Italy works on a 220V wiring system. Anyone using 120V appliances needs to obtain a transformer. Italian plugs have two prongs that are round, not flat; both adaptor plugs and transformers can be bought at the airport or at a local electrical or hardware store (*Elettricità* or *Casalinghi*).

EMBASSIES & CONSULATES All embassies are located in Rome, but the following countries have consulates in Naples: **US** (Piazza della Repubblica 2, ☎ 081/5838111; www.usis.it); **Canada** (Via Carducci 29, ☎ 081/401338; www.canada.it); **UK** (Via Crispi 122, ☎ 081/663511 or 081/663589; www.britain.it).

EMERGENCIES Dial ☎ 113 or 112 for the police; ☎ 118 for an ambulance; and ☎ 115 for a fire. For road emergencies dial ☎ 803-116.

HOSPITALS The most central hospital in Naples that provides 24-hour emergency care (*pronto soccorso*) is the **Policlinico,** Via Sergio Pansini (☎ 081/7461111), but a (less central) better option is the **Cardarelli,** Via Cardarelli 9, Vomero Alto (☎ 081/7471111).

For significant but non-life-threatening ailments, you can walk into most hospitals and get speedy care—with no questions about insurance policies, no forms to fill out, and no fees to pay. **Obviously it's still crucial to carry an appropriate travel health insurance policy.** EU citizens should take an EHIC card to be certain of free reciprocal health care; forms are available in the UK from Post Offices or at www.ehic.org.uk. Most hospitals in the Naples area will be able to find someone who speaks English.

HOLIDAYS Italian public holidays are as follows: 1 January, New Year's Day; 6 January, Epiphany (*La Befana*); Easter Monday (*Pasquetta*); 25 April, Liberation Day; 1 May, Labour Day; 2 June, Republic Day; 15 August, Feast of the Assumption (*Ferragosto*); 1 November, All Saints' Day; 8 December, Feast of the Immaculate Conception; 25 December, Christmas Day; 26 December, Boxing Day (*Santo Stefano*). In addition, Naples virtually closes down on 19 September for the Feast of San Gennaro, the city's patron saint. Many shops, businesses, and restaurants in Naples close for at least part of August.

INTERNET In larger cities and towns, Internet access is plentiful and most hotels now offer at least an Internet point for guests' use. WiFi is becoming increasingly common in hotels too, although you may have to pay for access. You will find plenty of Internet points and cafés in Naples and larger towns. Internet points in Naples include: **Internet Bar** (Piazza Bellini 74, ☎ 081/295237); **Clic Net** (Via Toledo 393, ☎ 081/5529370); **City Hall Café** (Corso Vittorio Emanuele 137a, ☎ 081/669400); **Internet**

Napoli (Piazza Cavour 146, ☎ 081/298877).

LANGUAGE Italian is the local language, but English is generally understood at most attractions, hotels, and restaurants that cater to visitors, as well as in many pharmacies. The Italians are very appreciative of any foreigner who attempts even a few words in their language; see 'Useful Phrases,' below.

LAUNDROMATS Public laundromats (*lavanderia a gettoni*) are extremely rare, but you can drop your laundry at most *tintoria* (dry cleaners) to have it washed, ironed, and folded. This is much cheaper than using hotel laundry services.

LOST PROPERTY Contact credit card companies the minute you realize your card has been stolen or lost. The following Italian numbers are free: **Visa** ☎ 800/819014; **Mastercard** ☎ 800/870866; **American Express** ☎ 800/872000. If you lose other valuables or suspect that they've been stolen, go to the nearest police station to make a statement (*denuncia*), which is required for insurance purposes. For luggage lost on a flight, go to the *ufficio bagagli smarriti* (lost luggage office) at the airport.

MAIL The mail service in Italy has improved enormously in recent years. Postcards (not in regular letter envelopes) pay a reduced rate, but are also the slowest. Now, all letters and postcards are delivered using the first class Posta Prioritaria service. Deliveries to the US should (and generally do) arrive within 4–8 days and within the EU but outside Italy within 3 days. Postcards and letters to the US and Canada weighing up to 20 grams (0.7 ounces) cost 0.85€; within Europe they cost 0.65€. You can buy stamps at all post offices and at *tabacchi* stores.

MONEY In January 2002, Italy switched from the lira to the euro. Coins come in denominations of 1, 5, 10, 20, and 50 cents, and 1€ and 2€; notes come in denominations of 5€, 10€, 20€, 50€, 100€, 200€, and 500€. Exchange rates fluctuate daily; to get the best rate, obtain cash from ATM machines (*bancomat*) or pay with your credit card where possible. Traveler's checks, although safe, are now almost obsolete. Try and avoid changing money at an exchange booth (*cambio*) or at a hotel; you will get a much better rate at a bank or ATM—but check overseas withdrawal fees before you leave home. All but the most modest restaurants and hotels accept plastic these days, although some don't take American Express or Diner's.

NEWSPAPERS & MAGAZINES The *International Herald Tribune* and *USA Today* are widely available, even in smaller towns. UK daily newspapers and the Sundays such as the *Times*, *Guardian*, *Telegraph*, and *Sunday Times* are available from larger newsstands in Naples and, in high season, from central newsstands in Sorrento, Positano, Amalfi, and Ischia. Note that these arrive the day after publication. *Time* and *Newsweek* are also widely available and larger newsstands stock US and UK editions of glossies such as *Vogue*, *Elle*, *Vanity Fair*, and *Cosmopolitan*.

The most widely read Italian newspapers are the Milan-based *Corriere della Sera* and Rome-based *La Repubblica*, both of which have Naples sections carrying events listings. For useful practical and tourist information plus listings, pick up a copy of the free, bimonthly *Qui Napoli* (published by the tourist office and also in English); for nightlife listings, look out for biweekly *Napoli Zero* (Italian only).

PARKING   Parking is a major problem in Naples and in most of the area described in this guide. If you're driving, note that parking spaces marked by blue lines carry a fee payable at street parking meters. Never park in front of a sign saying *passo carrabile*, or in areas with signs saying *sosta vietata* or *zona rimozione*. Disabled parking places are marked in yellow and are free (bring your badge from home). In Naples, unofficial attendants will offer to keep an eye on your car while it's parked. Though this is technically illegal, it's a system that works. Tip them 1€ when you collect the car.

SAFETY   Naples has received a lot of negative press in recent years, but although petty crime such as bag snatching and pickpocketing is common, you're extremely unlikely to encounter violent crime. Pickpockets and bag snatchers are particularly active in tourist areas and prey on the unwary, so keep your eyes open and take precautions. Leave expensive-looking jewelry and watches in the hotel safe. Carry your bag across your chest and don't hold lots of cash or credit cards. Don't keep wallets in back pockets. Keep handbags closed and never leave them on the back of a chair in a restaurant or bar. Be particularly careful in crowds. And don't worry!

SMOKING   Since the Italian anti-smoking laws came into force, smoking is banned in enclosed public spaces, except those with separate ventilated smoking areas. It's also banned on public transport. These rules aren't always respected, especially in anarchic Naples.

TIME ZONE   Campania is 6 hours ahead of US Eastern Standard Time and 1 hour ahead of Greenwich Mean Time. Daylight-saving time comes into effect in Italy each year from the last Sunday in March to the last Sunday in October.

TIPPING   Tipping in Italy is discretionary and not expected in many cases but is, however, appreciated when service merits it. In hotels, it's customary to tip the porter for carrying your bags or for parking your car and the maid who cleans your room. Anything from 5–10€ is fine; more to the maid if you stay longer. Restaurants may add 10–15% service to your bill; it should be listed under *servizio*. If in doubt, ask 'Èincluso il servizio?' If it isn't, add it yourself but leave cash on the table. If it is, leave a few coins for the poor waiter if you feel you've had good service. Taxi drivers will be happy if you round up the fare one or two euros, but won't make a fuss if you don't.

TOILETS   Airports, train stations, museums, and major archaeological areas and attractions all have toilets, often with attendants who expect to be tipped a nominal fee (0.50€ is fine). Public toilets are a bit of a rarity in Naples. If you're desperate, go into a bar; they usually let you use the facilities. Usually they're designated WC (water closet) and bear international symbols or the signs *donne/SIGNORE* (women) and *uomini/SIGNORI* (men). It's a good idea to carry tissues; toilet paper is not always included.

TOURIST OFFICES   Naples: Ente Provinciale del Turismo, Piazza dei Martiri 58 (☎ 081/4107211; www.eptnapoli.info), open Mon–Fri 9am–2pm; Azienda Autonoma di Soggiorno, Via San Carlo 9 (☎ 081/402394; www.inaples.it), open Apr–Oct Mon–Sat 9:30am–2pm & 3–7pm, Nov–Mar Mon–Sat 9am–1:30pm & 4:30–6:30pm; Piazza Gésu Nuovo (☎ 081/5523328), open Mon–Sat 9am–7pm, Sun 9am–2pm.

Sorrento: Via Luigi di Maio 35 (☎ 081/8074033; www.sorrento tourism.com or www.infosorrento. it), open May–Sept daily 8:30am–6:30pm, Oct–Apr Mon–Sat 8:30am–4pm.

Positano: Via del Saracino 4 (☎ 089/875067; www.azienda turismopositano.it), open June–Sept Mon–Sat 8am–2pm & 3–8pm, Oct–May Mon–Sat 8am–2pm.

Ravello: Via Roma 18b (☎ 089/857096; www.ravellotime.it), open Mon–Sat 9am–7pm.

Amalfi: Corso delle Repubblica Marinare 27 (☎ 089/871107; www.amalfitouristoffice.it), open May–Oct Mon–Sat 8:30am–1pm & 3–6pm, Sun 8:30–1pm; Nov–Apr closed Sat afternoon and Sun.

Ischia & Procida: Via A Sogliuzzo 72, Ischia Porto (☎ 081/5074211; www.infoischiaprocida.it), open Apr–Oct Mon–Sat 9am–2pm & 3–8pm.

Capri: Piazza Umberto I, Capri (☎ 081/8370634; www.capri tourism.com), open Apr–Sept Mon–Sat 8:30am–8:30pm, Nov–Mar Mon–Sat 9am–1pm & 3:30–6:30pm.

WATER In restaurants, most locals drink mineral water (either fizzy *gassata* or still *non-gassata*) with their meals. However, tap water is safe everywhere, as are public drinking fountains. Unsafe sources and fountains will be marked *acqua non potabile*. If in doubt, ask the locals; they'll give you a straight answer.

Naples & the Amalfi Coast: **A Brief History**

C. 800 B.C. Greeks from the island of Euboea establish a trading station on Ischia, which they call Pithekoussai. They travel to Cumae on the mainland where they set up vital trade links with the rest of the Mediterranean.

800–358 B.C. Campania becomes an important part of Magna Grecia, which will cover the whole of southern Italy; Cuma becomes the area's most powerful city.

600 B.C. The Cuman Greeks found Partenope over Monte Echia (behind Piazza del Plebiscito in modern Naples). In the meantime, the sophisticated and powerful Etruscans have been establishing colonies in the interior of Campania as far down as the river Sele, inland from Paestum. They make their capital in Capua.

524 AND 474 B.C. Battles are fought between rival Etruscans and Greeks at Cuma. Both conflicts are won by the Greeks but they are threatened by the Sannite hill tribes.

C. 470 B.C. The 'New City' of Neapolis is founded by the Greeks next to Partenope.

328 B.C. The Romans lay siege to Neapolis and take the city two years later.

273 B.C. Rome establishes a colony in Paestum.

194 B.C. The Romans re-found Pozzuoli with the name of Puteoli.

27 B.C. Roman Empire is established under Augustus. After years of civil wars and economic instability, Neapolis is once again a cultural center attracting writers, teachers, and holidaymakers.

A.D. 79 Vesuvius erupts, burying the wealthy towns of Pompeii, Herculaneum, and Stabiae.

5TH CENTURY The Roman Empire has slowly declined, and with it, Naples. Barbarian invaders (Goths and Vandals) pass through Campania challenging Naples.

476 The last Roman Emperor, Romulus Augustus (captured by Goth King Odoacer), dies and the Empire falls.

530 General Belisarius, sent by Byzantium Emperor Justinian, takes Naples.

554 Naples becomes a Duchy under the Byzantines. In the following centuries, Naples is besieged by a multitude of invaders including the Lombards from the north and Saracens from north Africa.

10TH & 11TH CENTURIES Amalfi's Maritime Republic reaches its apogee; it is allied with Byzantium.

1027 Lombard Prince Pandolf IV of Capua takes power in Naples but reigning Duke Sergio IV enlists help from the Normans and together they drive the Lombards out.

1062–77 The Normans increase their power (with help from France) taking Capua, Amalfi, and Salerno. They push into southern Italy.

1130 Norman Ruggiero II is crowned King of Sicily.

1139 Naples surrenders to Ruggero II, and becomes part of the Norman kingdom of Sicily with Palermo as its capital; Naples takes a back seat.

1194 The last of the Lombard line, Tancred, dies. The Kingdom of Sicily passes to the Holy Roman Emperor Henry of Swabia.

1214 Friedrich II, son of Henry, finally succeeds to the thrones of the Holy Roman Empire and southern Italy. While keeping his brilliant court in Palermo, he transforms Naples into a center of learning and excellence and builds a new university.

1266 The Angevins defeat the Swabians in the battle of Benevento, taking over the kingdom. Charles of Anjou (Carlo I) transfers the capital from Palermo to Naples. He builds the Castel Nuovo.

1282 The Vespri Siciliani uprisings: the abandoned Sicilians revolt against their Angevin Kings and Charles loses Sicily to the Aragonese.

1347–48 The Black Death wipes out one-third of the population of Italy.

1442 Alfonso 'The Magnanimous' of Aragon, King of Sicily, drives the Angevins out of Naples and the kingdom is reunited.

1494 Charles III of France occupies Naples but the following year, the city is restored to its Spanish king, Ferdinand II. Thus begins two centuries of hated, oppressive Spanish rule or, often, misrule.

EARLY 17TH CENTURY With a population of 300,000, Naples is Europe's biggest city.

1631 On December 16, Vesuvius erupts, killing over 3,000.

1647 Southern Italy rises against Spanish taxes and oppression in the Masaniello's Revolt, crushed after a year by the Spanish, who massacre 18,000.

1656 Plague leaves three-quarters of Naples' population dead, buried in mass graves.

1713 Habsburgs of Austria gain control of Naples after the Wars of the Spanish Succession.

1734 The kingdom of Naples passes to Bourbon rule; Don Carlos enters the city in triumph and the following year is crowned King Carlo III of the Kingdom of Sicily. Naples is reinstated as capital and thrives intellectually and culturally.

1737 Carlo builds the San Carlo opera house.

1748 Excavations are started in Pompeii.

1799 In Naples, insurrection leads to the establishment of the liberal but short-lived Repubblica Partenopea.

1806 After several battles, Naples is taken by the French under Joseph Bonaparte.

1816 The Bourbons take back the kingdom under the newly-titled King Ferdinand I of the Kingdom of the Two Sicilies.

1840 The road SS 163—the famous Amalfi Coast drive—is opened to traffic.

1860 On September 7, Garibaldi enters Naples; the city votes overwhelmingly to join a united Italy under Vittorio Emanuele II of Savoy.

1884 Naples is devastated by a cholera epidemic; it becomes increasingly poor. Between 1880 and 1914, mass immigration to America takes place.

1940 On November 1, Allied planes bomb Naples devastating the city and destroying many monuments.

1943 In the Quattro Giornate Napoletane, the Neapolitans themselves liberate their city from the Germans. The Allies arrive in a desperately impoverished city where the black market and the Camorra (the Neapolitan Mafia) thrived.

1946 The Italian Republic is officially established in Naples, although the city voted overwhelmingly to keep the monarchy. Vittorio Emanuele sails from Naples into exile.

1950s Naples grows explosively, with 80,000 dwellings built within a decade, many of them without planning permission. Corruption and crime are rife: Naples has reached its blackest hour.

1980 A violent earthquake kills 3,000.

1993 Left-wing Antonio Bassolino is elected mayor of Naples. A major cleanup, restoration, and anti-crime campaign begin.

1994 The G7 meeting is held in Naples.

1995 The historic center of Naples is included in the UNESCO list of World Heritage Sites. The archaeological areas of Pompeii, Herculaneum, and Torre Annunziata, as well as the Reggia of Caserta and the Amalfi Coast, are added in 1997.

2001 Bassolino steps down as Naples mayor and is succeeded by Rosa Russo Iervolino, the first woman to hold the post. She remains in office at the time of writing.

2005 In the early part of the year, a crime war between rival Camorra factions gets international press, but historic Naples is unaffected.

2007 In the latter part of the year, a crisis in Naples' trash collection system (largely controlled by the Camorra) provokes anger among residents and attracts international media attention. Rubbish piles up on the streets, but the *centro storico* is mainly spared.

2008 100,000 tonnes of trash has built up in Naples streets, and residents stage violent protests.

2009 In March, Neapolitans hold one of their biggest ever demonstrations against the Camorra.

Useful **Phrases**

Italian is a beautiful language, accompanied in situ with much gesticulation, at which the Neapolitans are particularly good. The locals will be delighted at any attempt, however faltering, you make to speak Italian. The only problem is that they might reply, and if they choose to do that in Neapolitan dialect, I can guarantee that you won't understand a word! Here are some key words and phrases to get you started.

Useful Terms & Phrases

ENGLISH	ITALIAN	PRONUNCIATION
Thank you	Grazie	graht-tzee-yey
You're welcome	Prego	prey-go
Please	Per favore	pehr fah-vohr-eh
Yes	Sì	see
No	No	noh
Good morning or Good day	Buongiorno	bwohn-djor-noh
Good evening	Buona sera	bwohn-ah say-rah
Good night	Buona notte	bwohn-ah noht-tay
How are you?	Come sta?	koh-may stah
Very well	Molto bene	mohl-toh behn-ney
Goodbye	Arrivederci	ahr-ree-vah-dehr-chee
Excuse me (to get attention)	Scusi	skoo-zee
Excuse me (to get past someone)	Permesso	pehr-mehs-soh
Where is. . . ?	Dovè. . . ?	doh-vey
the station	la stazione	lah stat-tzee-oh-neh
a hotel	un albergo	oon ahl-behr-goh
a restaurant	un ristorante	oon reest-ohr-ahnt-eh
the bathroom	il bagno	eel bahn-nyoh
To the right	A destra	ah dehy-stra
To the left	A sinistra	ah see-nees-tra
Straight ahead	Avanti (or sempre dritto)	ahv-vahn-tee (sehm-pray dreet-toh)
How much is it?	Quanto costa?	kwan-toh coh-sta
The check, please	Il conto, per favore	eel kon-toh pehr vohr-eh
When?	Quando?	kwan-doh
Yesterday	Ieri	ee-yehr-ree
Today	Oggi	oh-jee
Tomorrow	Domani	doh-mah-nee
Breakfast	Prima colazione	pree-mah coh-lahttzee-ohn-ay
Lunch	Pranzo	prahn-zoh
Dinner	Cena	chay-nah
What time is it?	Che ore sono?	kay or-ay soh-noh

ENGLISH	ITALIAN	PRONUNCIATION
Monday	**Lunedì**	*loo-nay-dee*
Tuesday	**Martedì**	*mart-ay-dee*
Wednesday	**Mercoledì**	*mehr-cohl-ay-dee*
Thursday	**Giovedì**	*joh-vay-dee*
Friday	**Venerdì**	*ven-nehr-dee*
Saturday	**Sabato**	*sah-bah-toh*
Sunday	**Domenica**	*doh-mehn-nee-kah*
January	**Gennaio**	*jehn-NAH-yoh*
February	**Febbraio**	*fehb-BRAH-yoh*
March	**Marzo**	*MAHR-tso*
April	**Aprile**	*ah-PREE-leh*
May	**Maggio**	*MAHD-joh*
June	**Giugno**	*JEWN-nyo*
July	**Luglio**	*LOOL-lyo*
August	**Agosto**	*ah-GOHS-toh*
September	**Settembre**	*seht-TEHM-breh*
October	**Ottobre**	*oht-TOH-breh*
November	**Novembre**	*noh-VEHM-breh*
December	**Dicembre**	*dee-CHEHM-breh*

Numbers

1	uno	*(oo-noh)*
2	due	*(doo-ay)*
3	tre	*(tray)*
4	quattro	*(kwah-troh)*
5	cinque	*(cheen-kway)*
6	sei	*(say)*
7	sette	*(set-tay)*
8	otto	*(oh-toh)*
9	nove	*(noh-vay)*
10	dieci	*(dee-ay-chee)*
11	undici	*(oon-dee-chee)*
20	venti	*(vehn-tee)*
21	ventuno	*(vehn-toon-oh)*
22	venti due	*(vehn-tee doo-ay)*
30	trenta	*(trayn-tah)*
40	quaranta	*(kwah-rahn-tah)*
50	cinquanta	*(cheen-kwan-tah)*
60	sessanta	*(sehs-sahn-tah)*
70	settanta	*(seht-tahn-tah)*
80	ottanta	*(oht-tahn-tah)*
90	novanta	*(noh-vahnt-tah)*
100	cento	*(chen-toh)*
1,000	mille	*(mee-lay)*
5,000	cinque mila	*(cheen-kway mee-lah)*
10,000	dieci mila	*(dee-ay-chee mee-lah)*

Index

See also Accommodations and Restaurant indexes, below.

Restaurant Index

Photo **Credits**